# Navigating Tomorrow

Rhona Post

Copyright © 2010 Rhona Post

All rights reserved.

ISBN: **0-9835080-1-1**
ISBN-13: **978-0-9835080-1-4**

DEDICATION

Navigating Tomorrow is dedicated to my many teachers and to my dearest friend, Walter Harris Gavin, who has stood by my side with a hammer and sword, pen and camera, drink and laughter these many years.

RHONA POST

# CONTENTS

|  | Prologue | 1 |
|---|---|---|
|  | Introduction | 4 |
| 1 | The More You Live The Less You Die | 24 |
| 2 | Seeing The Light | 28 |
| 3 | Simon Says | 34 |
| 4 | Let's Pretend | 46 |
| 5 | It's a Universal Thing | 54 |
| 6 | The House That Jack Built | 58 |
| 7 | Let's Play Doctor | 69 |
| 8 | Abracadabra | 77 |
| 9 | It's Like Riding a Bicycle | 95 |
| 10 | Sound Off | 100 |
| 11 | Practice, Practice, Practice | 109 |
|  | Appendix | 127 |
|  | Acknowledgements | 137 |

RHONA POST

# Prologue

**TO THE 2010 EDITION**

*Navigating Tomorrow* is a primer on how to start over, whether you're starting over voluntarily or starting over as the result of an event beyond or outside your control. Divorce to lay-offs, financial setbacks or the death of a loved one are all opportunities to start over, again.

The idea of reinventing the self is not new. As an instructor at the University of South Florida's Lifelong Learning Academy, I teach alongside men and women who have started over two and three times in their careers. What each person has in common is a commitment to learning. Is this their final career? Who knows? Time will tell.

At a recent breakfast meeting with teaching colleagues, we introduced ourselves, identifying major milestones in our careers and relationships. When it was my turn to speak, I felt a surge of emotion as I realized how fortunate I am to be living longer, doing more, and trying more things than even my parents, before me. When my father was approaching sixty, he felt his life was over. I do not feel the same way, nor did any one person in the room express that concern. In fact, we were all excited to keep going, as if we do not have sufficient time to engage in all the many creative projects on our lists.

From time to time, we come across a tool or concept that has many applications. For example, I have used a screwdriver to both screw and dislodge nails, remove gum from the bottom of my show, widen the space between metal and the wood to which it adhered, etc.,

The tool I am introducing in Navigating Tomorrow is akin to a screwdriver because as you become proficient with it, you will find other applications for it.

Initially, I used this tool to reinvent my own life after experiencing a great loss. Feeling very unsteady in myself, I was searching for something to hold onto while I figured out my next steps. I needed some way to re-set my internal compass, to reduce my sense of vulnerability and powerlessness. As I began experimenting with the three-step tool, I observed myself gaining strength, translating varied insights I had gained into action.

At the same time I was re-setting my course I became more sensitive to how other people experienced their heartbreak and loss, whether the loss was a result of a natural disaster, a loved one, or even the loss of a position. Some people popped back up to play again, while others kept going downhill resigning themselves to a fate over which they had no power. They gave up; I kept fighting for my happiness.

What emerged for me during the research and writing of this book was the knowledge that each of us wants to be happy, no matter what situation we find ourselves. With my coaching background, I could see how taking this tool into a business setting would help my clients see which facet of their business required attention. For that reason, I included both examples of personal and business reinvention. Often business owners or leaders will press the "wrong button" with employees, focusing individual or team efforts on areas that result in greater distress in the workplace. The three step tool helped re-orient managers' thinking to focus on the right issue at the right time for the right reasons.

Whether the need to reinvent is sparked by personal or professional loss, we still follow the same three steps. We want a picture or vision of what is worth doing so that we can move ourselves in the direction of our dreams. We'll need a structure or template to help us translate our ideas into something concrete and we have to identify and develop the core competencies required to fulfill the vision. Working with a coach helps us get unstuck from vantage points that hamper our performance, as well as learning how to get out of our own way so that we can actually have the life we dream.

By answering the questions of when, where, how, what, and why we use each facet of the tool makes the whole concept easier to implement. My intention is to provide the blueprint you can use to cultivate your internal navigation system.

*The ideas you will find throughout this book are timeless. It is my hope that like me you will find yourself going back to them time and again.*

Rhona Post

RHONA POST

# Introduction

**REINVENTING THE WHEEL OR CHANGING THE TIRE?**

## Richard Barnett, Ph.D. Retired NBA Basketball, New York Knicks

*"The whole marketplace and the idea of work have changed. People don't go to corporations and return with a gold watch. You've got to be able to reinvent yourself. You have to be able to work at home, use the Internet, use technology, do whatever you have to do to survive and seek your dreams in a broader world.*

*The ax is coming unless you work for yourself. The greatest transition I ever made, I decided I don't work for anybody. I am an independent contractor selling my services. I teach professional athletes the independent contract theory. You have to be able to work for yourself and do it successfully. You've got to marry your dreams with reality. Inevitably the day always comes when you are replaced. You have to be prepared. Everybody has to meet that day."*

### Reinvention:

<u>Invent:</u>   To conceive of or devise.
<u>Invention:</u>   The act or process of inventing.
<u>Reinvent:</u>   To re-conceive. To devise for oneself again.
<u>Reinvention:</u>   The act or process of inventing a new device, method or process from study and experimentation anew or again.

## *ICON KEY*

📁   Coaching Exercise

✏   Practices

It is not necessary to go through major life changes to reinvent the self. Although we grew up hearing "necessity is the mother of invention" we do not need to have our backs against a wall to change how we are or how we live our lives. Crisis is a great motivation for some people. For others, redesigning their lives becomes a possibility not out of crisis but out of despair or emptiness. They have done everything right and yet they still feel empty. Some people build their lives around change, facing each roadblock along the way as an exciting challenge to figure out and conquer. They are driven by their desire to keep learning about who they are.

When I first began writing *Navigating Tomorrow*, I wanted to talk to people who had experienced the impact emotionally, physically, intellectually and spiritually of rapid change in their lives. Not only was I interested in exploring our reactions and responsiveness to change, as a result of job loss or corporate merger, relationship loss, sudden illness or business failure, I wanted to know what elements, if any, supported their transition from loss to something new. I knew many of us bounced back from loss, while others continued the downward spiral.

Everyone who has experienced loss resulting from change does not have a game plan for managing the changes. All of us will confront a situation that pulls the rug out from under us. We may think we know what we are doing or we believe our actions will take care of us through change, but as I shared my findings with friends, colleagues and clients, I realized two things:

**1.** People from all walks of life are searching for more effective ways to manage the changes that occur in their lives, and

**2.** It doesn't matter what game you are playing in life, the elements required to successfully navigate change are the same.

Initially, I was going to concentrate my research by interviewing retired professional athletes. They represented a group of men and women whose foundation is so well rooted in one particular way of life, that I was curious to learn how they survived or even thrived after sports. How did they begin a new life, after they had dedicated so much of their lives to one game? As I engaged in conversations with retired players, I learned successful *Reinventer*s share three similar elements.

I knew that mastering change required not only a physical shift in how I lived in myself, but also that I had to re-frame my identity to be congruent with how I wished to live. No matter whom I interviewed for this book, what we shared in common was that we each spent time learning about ourselves, discovering or uncovering what was important, learning about the traits we wished to cultivate as well as how we wished to live. We translated this new vision into action by designing or developing structures that would house or support our picture of our lives. Finally, we had to develop the skills and knowledge necessary to accomplish our goals.

Some of my best interviews about reinventing the self were conducted with three ex-convicts, people most of us will never meet or know because we have dismissed them as felons. They spoke reinvention from their hearts. Not only did they transform the quality of their lives; they transcended their own negative labels. They didn't simply change from being convicted felons to ex-convicts. Rather they invented a new context for themselves that allowed them to create new labels for themselves, labels that increased their self-confidence as they created new lives after incarceration. In fact, they were no longer their labels. Yes, they acknowledged they had done unlawful acts, but they learned through self -discovery that they were not the unlawful acts they did. Although I may have started out interviewing the experts in reinvention, I ended up dialoguing with a diverse group of people, from all walks of life, whose stories became the foundation for my reinvention theory.

Reinvention requires not simply a change in venue, or a change in how we do what we do; reinvention requires the creation of something new. All Creators need tools. I'm going to guide you how to view yourself as *creators* of your new vision as well as provide the coaching materials you can use to reinvent your lives. If, on the other hand, you are coaching a client who has experienced loss resulting from change, who is stuck trying to move forward, you can use this book as a coaching resource.

Each chapter includes a combination of narratives, excepts from men and women who have navigated change, as well as lots of short, quick, yet challenging exercises that will strengthen your competence to create a new vision for yourself.

I created what I call *The Navigating Tomorrow Tool* (Fig. 1) to use in the reinvention process. It is a triangle whose sides are Vision, Structure or System and Skills or Competencies. Each side is defined. By the time you complete this book, you will be more skillful reinventing your life, at work or at home. The three elements that an individual uses to reinvent the self are the same three elements an individual uses to reinvent an organization. *Navigating Tomorrow* is not a fix it book. *Navigating Tomorrow* is a toolbox that strengthens your competence to create a new vision for your life.

I have learned ten great lessons from writing this book.

1. Reinvention of the self does not happen in a vacuum. We need help and/or guidance from others to reinvent our lives
2. We can reinvent our lives and our organizations more than once.
3. Figuring out what is worth doing with our lives or our organizations is a great first step in this process.
4. Vision, structure and skills are the tools upon which to rely for mastering change.
5. Anyone who dreams about how he/she wants his/her life to be-can reinvent himself/herself.
6. No matter how old we are, or how stuck in our ways we have become, with a little help we can transform our relationship to ourselves, to others and to life.
7. Reinvention of the self is not a mental exercise.
8. If we start with the end in mind, we will go a long way reinventing our lives.
9. Many times along the way, we will fail and succeed in our efforts.
10. The more we bring our lives into alignment with "who we are" and what matters to us the more peace and joy we

experience.

## 📁 Coaching Tip: (see Appendix)

Inventing or reinventing a life requires reflection and action.

You get to explore and interact with questions like:

1. What do I want my life to include?
2. What are the kinds of projects I would like to be doing?
3. What do I want my life to look like, to feel like?
4. What are the kinds of people or projects that zap my energy?
5. What have I done in the past that has made me happy?
6. If I had one year left to live, what would I do?

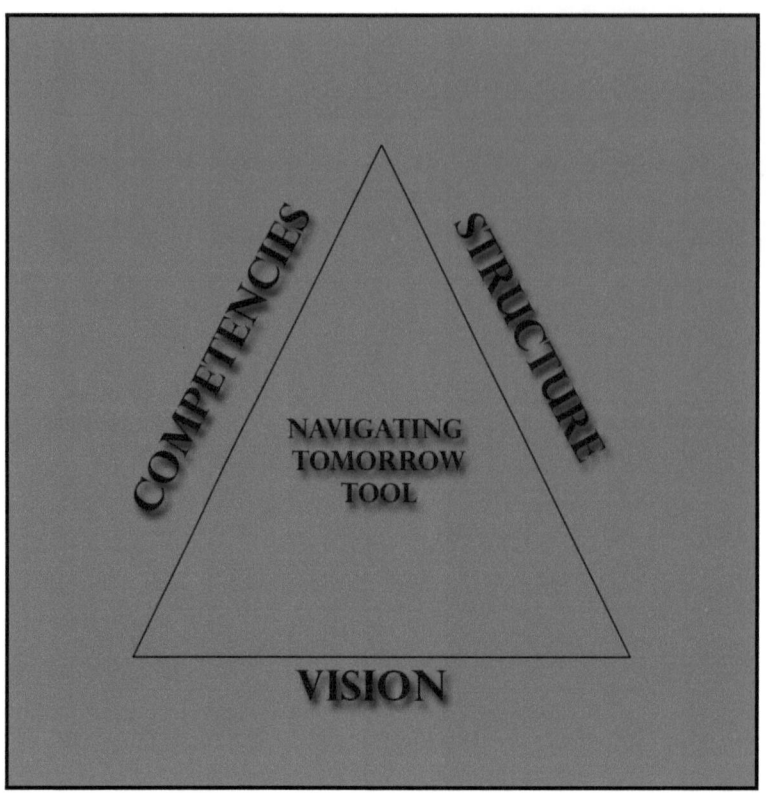

Fig. 1

**Melissa McNair Bennett, Integrated Life Practices CEO**

*"I see reinvention as a stance or relationship with life. It goes beyond having an awareness; it is almost an ability to unglue yourself form certain things that have kept you stuck in life. Reinvention is a constant dialogue with oneself in life. Does this value fit with who and what you are in life? It's a dialogue that goes with facts, events and relationships. I see transformation as taking a part of yourself that feels like grit and through processes like workshops, coaching, reading, you can remove the grit to see the pearl in yourself."*

**Mitchell Johnson—National Football League, retired**
**Had long career in financial world, retired from Sally Mae, now tinkers with his stock portfolio.**

*"The biggest thing is you have to want to change, have to have the desire to change. Easy thing is to continue staying in the same thing you were doing, where you were comfortable. Doing something different takes work, courage and desire Lots of times you don't know where you are going to end up as you start these journeys but you do know you are not going to stay where you are."*

## Coaching Tip:
Ask Yourself:
How will you know when you are doing the right thing or doing the things right?

Reinvention might sound like a lot of work, but I found that when people are faced with the prospect of finding new jobs, creating new careers, or starting over after any major loss they actually enjoy the process of self-discovery. We may not relish the idea of starting over, we may actually find ourselves bemoaning our fate for some time, but even as we mourn our losses, we are still moving forward. A focused approach to reinvention allows us to discover ourselves in a whole new way. We are not beholden to old pictures of ourselves. In fact, coaching serves as a vehicle for change, a backboard against which our clients can practice new skills. What's the downside to reinventing? All efforts take time, money and support. We do not reinvent in a vacuum.

Believing that you can change your life is a great first step. Scraping away the layers of our lives we begin seeing how we have lived. We roil between amazement and sadness as we clear away the cobwebs. For each step we take we find something to cherish. Our hope is that we will find what we have been missing or discover that which we cherish in ourselves as we keep propelling ourselves forward.

## Practice:
Scared To Try?

Join the crowd. We're all scared to look under the surface of how we live. We keep thinking we will find that part of ourselves that is most shameful or most hateful. The key to success with this practice is to be gentle, practicing kindness for yourself each step of the way.

## Exercise:
Ask Yourself:

If you could paint your life, what elements would you include on the canvas?

What images would the canvas hold?

What mood would be evoked in you when you look at the picture of your life?

Changing the self happens in community where and where we feel safe to "reveal" ourselves. Our learning community provides trust, respect and honesty so that we can effectively gauge our progress. When we listen to others share their pain or joy, we feel less separate. Within the community, we take risks with our selves, especially when the results we get inspire us to keep looking, experimenting, failing and succeeding.

How do you know when it is time to reinvent your life? There are usually three keys to knowing when things are not working right for you.

**Keys:**

1. You know you are in trouble. Your back is up against the wall and you need help.
2. You have accomplished your goals, have a sense of worth, but yet you keep singing an old refrain: Is this all there is? Something seems to be missing and you don't know what or how to change.
3. You realize that life is grand. You want more. You want to keep your lead in the game. You know you can't do the work on your own. You need a coach who will hold the commitment with you, pushing, prodding, encouraging, and supporting your passion to achieve.

> **"He is letter to everyone,**
> **You open it.**
> **It says,**
> **Live.**          Rumi

## William Dennis Turner, Golden Gloves Boxer, Ex-Convict, Fully Free

*"What does it take to reinvent the self? There are a lot of people who fail. They say that prison bars do not a prison make. You could be in your own little prison. It takes a willingness to want to succeed. It takes someone inquisitive. Provoking a person to think and take a good look. Maybe we don't need to know the answers but we do need to ask ourselves the questions. A lot of times we come out of prison and the first thing we do is hope for success and that never happens. In our efforts dealing with mainstreaming we have to cushion our transition before we are released, before we pursue a particular career field or specific goal. We have to mentally prepare for coming home. Not the balloons, not the confetti, or the*

band.

*I have to tell myself that I cannot catch up. I realized when I was incarcerated that there are quite a lot of people who never take a look at themselves They look inside themselves to see what they are made of, and they're looking to see what kinds of skills they have and how thick or how profound their poetry is within themselves, but they never look at the fact that they have mountains inside.*

*It is rough leaving prison because you have to program yourself to do well with what you have and maintain the direction in which you are heading. If you have no tools, you need to get some. You are your own mechanic's box but you have to have tools. Without tools you cannot be your own mechanic."*

## Gordon Graham, Ex-Convict, Now CEO of Graham and Associates, Correctional Training Company

*"Reinvention is almost doing a complete overhaul of the engine that drives you. You develop a frame of reference inside yourself. If you are going to truly reinvent yourself, then you have to go back and really do some stuff with those mind maps (inner voices). Change and evaluate some of the things that used to be the truth for you but are no longer relevant. We operate automatically on a lot of information that is no longer relevant to who we are. You have to ask yourself, "Where did this information come from? Who put these barriers in my thinking? Are these ideas still relevant for me?"*

# Introduction

**FALLING FROM GRACE**

*My life is my message*
　　　　　Mahatma Gandhi

As I began interviewing men and women about their experience with loss, whether the loss was a career, a relationship or their freedom, I realized I was hearing similarities in the stories shared by my clients and the interviewees. Both groups employed many of the same methods to survive and thrive after a major loss.

How people tell their stories might differ but the bumps and bruises, the emotional highs and lows experienced are very much the same. We share common beliefs about life, remains the same as current text..

Even United States federal agencies are realizing that goal setting and accomplishment is a crucial element to their organizational success. What seems to be creating more tension for people is our tenaciousness to hold onto our beliefs even when these beliefs no longer serve us.

**Core Beliefs Include:**
- We think we will live forever.
- We believe that if we play the game well, we will remain on the team.
- We define ourselves by what we do. We are football players, we are advertising executives, or we are supervisors in organizations. We doctors, lawyers or Indian Chiefs.
- The game we play is the only game in town.
- We develop a culture with particular customs and habits around the game we play. We take on specific roles, responsibilities, rules, friendships, and other games while we play our game. Our Game becomes institutionalized with its own set of controls, habits, customs etc., defining our actions.
- We like to know where we stand in the game because not knowing makes us very uncomfortable. And we hate being uncomfortable.

- We tell ourselves we will learn another game while we are still playing this game because we know no game lasts forever.
- We wish we had the time, energy and money to learn another game while we are still playing, but we don't want to lose our focus.
- We tell ourselves we can learn a new game after this one is over.
- We don't have to play our best. We can simply show up for the game and say, " That's good enough!"
- We hold others responsible when our game is over.
- We resist giving up the game(s) we've been playing, even when the game is over.
- We think the big game of life is over when we lose a small game.
- We hold memories of how we played like movies.
- We watch a lot of reruns.

I wrote this book because I don't want other people to go in the many circles I did when my game was over. I wish I could say that there is one simple way to navigate and survive the changes we all will experience. There are many ways to navigate change and all these paths require the same three ingredients: Vision, structure and skills.

Reinventing focuses on closing the gap between what we want in life, or from life and what we currently have. We cannot simply do the same thing somewhere else. The somewhere else may no longer exist by the time we get there. Worse, the skills and knowledge we've accumulated may no longer be acceptable, or even applicable.

## Len Elmore—National Basketball Association, retired

*"The way I looked at it was, always prepare for the fall! It's such a turn-on. You know the saying, "Expect the worse, and hope for the best?"*

*In basketball, the fall is inevitable. When you feel that cement below you, you can fall and have that rude shock or you can place cushions down. Place as many cushions as you can while you are still playing. Cushions like: education, network development, community participation, and reputation. Maintain a stellar reputation. Without that reputation, none of the other stuff really works!"*

By the time we are in our forties, we have experienced a wide range of emotions, accumulated a wealth of experience, and amassed at least one household full of souvenirs. Each birthday has brought happiness and sadness--happiness for what I have achieved, sadness for what I have not achieved or have lost.

I don't think I became conscious to the experience of falling apart until my father died in 1986. The year following his death was one of dark shadows draping my day-to-day existence. With his passing, I lost the opportunity to talk with him, to hear his voice. Although I had no regrets about my life with him, I certainly missed his presence. His death was my first significant experience with change beyond my control. I began noticing that attached to the event called death was a letting go process. I was incredibly lonely. I felt wounded. Although people knew of my dad's passing, we did not spend much time in conversation about my experience with his loss. I simply wandered around my life waiting for the wound to heal.

My second experience with major loss due to major change was the demise of my 14-year friendship with Trixie.

I met Trixie when I was thirty-two. We quickly fell into line with one another. We hung out a lot, sharing our innermost secrets, our hopes and fears, our dreams. An unlikely partnership took shape. We became fast friends both at work and outside. We grew into each other's lives. When she moved south to live with her boyfriend, we stayed in touch. I became a confidant. There was a foundation underneath us. Over time we became a custom, a norm in each other's existence upon which we continued to build our relationship.

This custom became something upon which we both depended. I spent all major holidays at her house. Even minor holidays became an opportunity to get together. I became a third wheel in her marriage, a fourth daughter in her family, a sister to her husband. I became linked to a family that provided love, support, nourishment, and care. In many ways it became difficult to define our roles with one. We expected to stay together always. Without really thinking about what we were building, we just kept constructing our lives around the traditions and habits we formed. This devotion to our friendship provided security, relevance and joy.

Our history seemed to cement our future. Just like someone who works in the same company for years, I believed that by having this institution called friendship with Trixie, I would receive certain benefits, both in the short and long term. To feel a part of something or someone bigger than yourself is exhilarating. I did not want this part of my life to end.

What a surprise when Trixie cut me from her life. Her ten-year marriage was dissolving, and she decided to terminate our relationship. I was pulled between her and her husband, even as she left to start over again with someone else. There was no room for debate, discussion, or reconsideration. This building called Friendship came crashing down on my head. I can still playback those last few minutes on the telephone. My whole being came alive as if I were saying goodbye to someone dying in my arms. We were suspended in this one final moment; then we hung up the phones. I felt tremors in every part of my being. A major life change began that day as I realized that I had to sever my ties.

As I began disengaging from the relationship, I realized how many ways I had integrated this friendship into my day- to- day existence. We talked daily for years. I did not realize the degree to which I had come to rely on my dear friend.

For the first weeks I was mentally and psychologically numb. Even my body reacted quite strangely. Often I was fatigued, worn out by my own sadness. My mind routinely replayed our conversations. My head grew weary of questioning, "Why is this happening to me? What did I do wrong?" I was scared about what would happen to me without her. I blamed myself for this huge loss; I prayed that she would notice the emptiness, call to reconnect. She never called again.

This kind of finality is scary because we just don't suddenly stop what we are doing or how we are doing what we are doing because someone or something has decided to change direction. Our feelings are still intact even if the relationship or job is over. We still love the game we were playing. It took me several years to accept the ending of our story. I always wanted a different ending than the one I received. No matter how well I rationalized Trixie's decision to terminate the friendship, I always held hope that she would somehow find me again. I had to keep reminding myself that her decision was hers and not mine. Her decision did not mean there was something wrong with me. But I had to work at this thinking.

The loss of this friendship gave me the chance to grieve deeply. I think that is what I noticed most as I thought about writing this book. It was my grief that I shared with others. It was my sensitivity to others' sadness about their losses that inspired me to look at innovative ways to start over.

In the beginning of any major life transition, we engage in endless bouts of self-talk that either lectures or lambastes us with a round of 'you should have, Why didn't you? You ought to, How could you, Now what?' or 'Why is this happening to me?'

The hours we spend in self-criticism promotes greater distress emotionally, physically, spiritually, and intellectually, because we have no real answers to why something has happened or why someone we love has done something so alien or mysterious. Would understanding her thinking have eased my pain? Temporarily maybe, but the bottom line was that we ended a fourteen year relationship in a fifteen minute phone call.

At what point do we stop grieving? I think we stop when we stop. Like the ice melting as the temperature rises, the lake thaws. Eventually I accepted this new reality.

I believe we can reduce the time we spend in self-inflicted pain by developing ourselves to be islands of strength. Not that we become impenetrable or totally protected from hurt, rather we can develop a template for our lives that will support us more effectively as we weather storms, either the self-inflicted storms or the ones inflicted on us just because. The more we can live from what we hold dear, the more space we have to succeed and fail, allow others to succeed and fail, and in general, be more at ease in ourselves. We cannot control others nor can we change anyone except ourselves.

## Maureen Bunyan---Former Anchor, Channel 9, Washington DC Now anchoring the Evening & Late night newscasts on WJLA-TV, Washington, DC

*"Society doesn't encourage us to find meaning in pain and suffering. Therefore we don't want to find meaning in it for anybody else. We reject people who are in pain. We look at people who do accept pain as saints. If you are in pain you go to a minister or rabbi or psychiatrist because they are the experts in dealing with pain. For example, when I was leaving Channel 9, I spoke to hundreds of people and I heard so much fear in other peoples' voices, in their comments. Especially people who were in my own profession, because they were relating what happened to me to themselves. On the other hand many of them had gone through similar experiences to mine, but they were not leaving their jobs. So, there was fear and guilt. They were wondering, 'If I were to do that…. or Would I be able to do what Maureen did and then if I did what Maureen did, would I fall into a bottomless pit and not get back out again?'*

*So we fear the future. We all know losses happen to everybody. We could learn so much more about how to cope with loss ourselves if we could observe others. But too often we throw each other out of the way instead of bringing each other in."*

In the middle of the transition from a shared life to a life without my best friend, Trixie, I started to listen more carefully to my clients. Behind their stories were strong emotions of fear and resentment as they came to terms with the many upheavals in their lives. At the time I began writing, I noticed more people in flux, more agencies grappling with decreased budgets, and fewer resources. We all take for granted that we will play the game forever, or until we choose to leave. I think I feel the same way about death. I will go when I am ready, and not one day before. How arrogant or silly I am. Whether the game is good or bad, the relationship positive or negative, we hate like hell to see it end. It takes us no time to get comfortable where we sit. I am starting to realize this is not such a human foible. My two cats will find comfortable perches wherever they are. They just want to be comfortable; that desire dictates where they will nap for the hour or sleep for the night. We all want to feel comfortable. Life itself can be our battleground, so finding comfort where and when we can takes precedence. There is nothing wrong with wanting to feel comfortable. It's just when the rug gets pulled out we fall apart.

Some of my public sector coaching clients were confused and even frustrated by decisions they had no role in making but which affected their futures. They were angry about losing control of their offices, their jobs, or even their careers. Whether we are senior executives, new players on a team, or recently separated from our spouse/partner, what we have in common is our lack of preparation for the fall. We all tell ourselves that if we continue to do our best, we will be okay.

Most of us are unskilled when it comes to starting a new game in life. Even when we are experts in our fields, when faced with transition, we are novices. We don't like endings of things. We don't like grieving for what we have loved and lost.

Vocal acknowledgement of loss enables us to move forward. My openness about how the demise of a long-term relationship was affecting my day-to-day life allowed others to both support me in my grief and share their own experiences. I felt like I was waking up. It's like buying a new car. You drive out of the dealership and for the next two weeks every other car you see on the road is like the one you just purchased. I was not alone in my suffering. Although there is an undertow to change that can pull you down, other times, the same current keeps us buoyant, floating towards what's next. If we can remember to stop fighting the current, we will be carried with greater ease towards what's next.

I learned to stop fighting the current. Every time I questioned or fought against what had happened to me, I sank beneath the surface, came up sputtering, choking, grasping for air. By slowly learning to let go of the anger and sadness about what had happened to me, I began feeling lighter, staying afloat, and could more easily extend to others. I felt less isolated in my own grief.

# Section One: Vision

**CHAPTER ONE:**

# The More You Live the Less You Die

## *What Does Having a Vision Do?*

Every person and every organization can have a vision. Your vision may intensify or alter over time, but it lives inside us waiting to be brought forward. A personal vision speaks to who we say are and what we say is worth doing. Nothing more. Nothing less. You can only cultivate and live from your own personal vision. You can support others to cultivate and farm their own personal visions. But my vision is mine and yours is yours.

When I first began managing a leadership training operation my supervisor suggested I write what a successful leadership organization would look like, and how I wanted to be known in that organization. Each day he asked, "What would you see? What would others see?". He suggested I record my writing and listen to it daily. Why? I wanted to know? He laughed as he exited my office. "It will take no time at all for you to forget why you are here. You will get derailed often," he promised, "listening to the taped vision statement will bring you back to your sense of purpose".

I thought the idea valid but of course I believed that if I knew in my heart what was worth doing I wouldn't need to be reminded. Was I ever wrong! Every time the wind blew a storm in the leadership training operation, I reacted adversely. My vision and everything I stood for, toppled. After several months, I decided to make a taped recording of my vision. When the waters of life are calm it's easy to remember why you are doing what you do; the real test is when you can hold on to your vision in the middle of a storm. Each time I listened, my spirit felt refreshed, as if there was some place in myself where I could go for safety and inspiration.

*Why is figuring out who you are so critical?* We're all looking for ways to steady ourselves in a world that is changing at a much faster rate than we can keep up with. Downsizing, restructuring, layoffs, illness, death, divorce, not to mention our own fears about what will happen to us, creates tremendous instability.

By identifying and bringing to life my own personal vision I have fortified myself in a world that is both alien and exciting. Knowing and dedicating my actions to bringing forth my dreams is the best revenge for successfully navigating constant change.

### The benefits of living from one's vision include:

*Serenity.* You become more at ease with yourself as you develop clarity about who you really are.

*Focus.* You see a purpose to your life as defined by your vision. When your focus blurs you simply plug back into your purpose (vision).

*Joy.* You experience a sense of aliveness in yourself that allows you to connect to yourself, others and to life.

*Sadness.* You allow yourself to feel both happy and sad. You do not hide from yourself.

*Continuous Performance Improvement.* As the diverse fragments of your life become integrated you feel better about yourself. Because you feel better, you are open to new possibilities that will sustain this emotion. You keep looking for ways to improve.

*Teaching Others.* The more you live from what you say is worth doing the easier it becomes to share yourself with others. Joy is contagious.

*Respect.* As you begin to live from what you say is worth doing in life you find space in yourself to let others be who they are in life. You no longer want to fight people; rather you want to be with people.

*Community:* You are drawn to others who are on the same path. In this community everyone is welcome.

*Gratefulness.* You have finally come home to yourself, not some version of yourself that you made up long ago, not some version of yourself you let others create for you somewhere along the line. You are grateful for each day that you live.

### Woody Fitzhugh   PGA Tour. Woody's Golf Range, Virginia

*"What guided me was my burning desire to be as good as I could be in golf. All my actions were related to the goal which was to get as good as I could get. I never thought starting as late as I did that I would ever be good enough to get into*

*the PGA tour. Most of those guys start when they are seven or eight years old. I started playing when I was twenty. I am not the most talented person in the world, either. I have moderate talent, but I had a huge work ethic and would just hit balls all day. I had two years in a row where I practiced and played every single day of the year, no matter what the weather was like. In the winter, I would just hit the ball and go find it out in the snow. Tee up on a big pile of snow. Just played and practiced every day."*

CHAPTER TWO:

# Seeing The Light

*A vision is a dream. A possibility. Before we think it (vision), it does not exist. We sense, experience, see, or even think a vision in our minds. When the experience of thinking or sensing our vision integrates with our whole being, from body to soul, we know we have found the god in our selves.*

## *Why Is Having A Vision Important?*

As you discover your true self you can't pretend that the self you are uncovering is someone else. You can turn away from yourself but a soul freed is a genie out of the bottle. There is no going back to the self you were. The past is over.

Sometimes I choose a dream to bring to life or sometimes a dream chooses me. If I'm lucky, I will spend my life living my dreams. I will have the chance to play to win, and the chance to be my own coach, coaching my performance in life. What are the benefits?

**Vision Benefits:**

- A blueprint to what's important in your life.
- Inner Peace. When all else fails or when all else succeeds, you always have the connection to self. Inner peace is our own sanctuary, where we can create, renew ourselves, lick our wounds, review our actions, or simply rest. Inner peace means we are home

At different points in time we may choose to follow the hit or miss theory of life, which means we are basically thrown or moved from one life event to another, always in search of that elusive peace and happiness. It's like setting sail without a course or direction. Most of us live this way. I am not saying that we don't set and achieve goals. We do. Hearing what our inner voice communicates requires quiet and for some of us, peace and quiet. We believe that the actions we're taking are consistent with our purpose in life, yet we still find we're not happy. Having a vision of what is worth doing serves as a propeller. That way we're moving forward in the direction of what we say is important. Designing a life around my personal vision was a result of working with an executive coach. Most of us tend to move or glide from one event to the next, hoping that the actions we take will net us good results in terms of making money, prestige, stability, relationships or all of it. I am not knocking this level of accomplishment, but we're here to examine the value and benefits of linking who we are with what we do.

Living from a personal or organizational vision produces a desire and ability to stand steady, even in the face of obstacles. My vision is bigger than what I can "make happen" today or tomorrow. The bigger the vision the greater the rewards. Course the opposite holds true as well: the bigger the vision, the greater are the risks! When living from a vision statement, we can more easily identify the specific commitments worth undertaking. There is a correlation between what I stand for, the actions I take, and the results I achieve. My vision becomes integral to who I am as a human being, and how I wish to live in the world.

I am not suggesting that all vision seekers are steady on their feet. We can still be tossed when storms hit. However, we quickly regain our balance to get back on the path of what we have declared is worth accomplishing. This is what living effectively is all about. It is not a straight shot from vision declaration to vision achievement. In fact for many people, the process of declaring, designing and fulfilling their vision becomes a lifelong journey. People who dedicate themselves to the adventure of self-exploration are always happier than those who follow the hit or miss theory of life. The more we live from our vision the more we live.

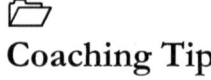
## Coaching Tip

***Never lose sight of your vision, and be willing to dance with life.***

The same way we think about an architect designing and building our dream house, we can engage in the conversation of designing a life or redesigning a person. Redesign requires several ingredients that we will explore at length in this book:

- Willingness to look and assess yourself.

- Courage to observe and change that which you say is worth changing.
- Strength to persevere.
- Faith in yourself and in something bigger than self.
- Time. Design work takes time.
- Network of support. No dream is birthed without the help of others.
- A personal/professional effectiveness coach.
- Patience. Building a new you takes time.
- Kindness for yourself and others.
- Willingness to play. Invention is not always hard work.

*"They must advance step by step, accustoming their inner eyes to a keener light before they can endure the dazzle of new truths, and they cannot be turned toward a good life except by their delights. For it is in these delights that keep them free and at last give them power to choose."*
**Helen Keller**

## Practice: Seeing What Is Underneath the Surface

### Instructions:

Spend five to ten minutes a day writing or dictating thought about your ideal work or home environment. Talk about the kinds of experiences you would be having in this ideal environment. Talk about the feelings, sensations, results, products, amount of money you would be earning, etc. Give yourself free rein to imagine this "ideal" life. After two weeks of writing, go back through your notes, and using a highlighter pen highlight the passages that strike a chord of interest. Then use the next two weeks to write how your life currently looks.

After four weeks of writing, ask yourself these five questions:

1. What have you learned about yourself in this process?
2. What actions, if any, will you take to help you close the gap between your ideal picture and your current reality?
3. What could get in the way?
4. What strategies can you put into place now to close the gaps so you will overcome the obstacles in the path?
5. What will closing the gap(s) require in terms of support from family or friends? Repeat questions #2-4.

*"Real meditation begins when you open your eyes..."*
**Hilda**

If you are not ready to jump into a practice but are curious about the concept of a vision, its usefulness or application in your life, why not begin exploring? Curiosity allows us to be playful without worrying that we have to return with "something". We can look at many options; study what is known and unknown, new or not yet experienced. Exploring provides the groundwork for building. Being curious allows for many answers, new questions, and the possibility of seeing something I could not see because I was so concerned about finding the solution to my vision problem. By removing the problem solution label to reinventing the self, I have some space to simply play. As you gather information, you will begin to see more clearly what actions you can take. And it is not necessary to act upon the information you've uncovered. Often, just sitting with the information will be enough to quiet the incessant need to have answers.

## Coaching Tip
## Conducting Your Vision Inquiry:

When I met James Flaherty, Founder of New Ventures West, he asked several questions at the start of our coaching program. These questions provided a foundation from which I could re-design my life. No one had ever asked us to reflect on the kind of life we thought would be worth living. Many of us have not explored or cultivated specific qualities that we admire in others. James gave us permission to view ourselves as a canvas upon which we could create our vision.

Although some of the projects identified in this process took many years to accomplish, we realized that if we died in the middle of doing these practices and projects, at least we could say we'd been in love with our lives!

Think of a practice as a way to strengthen a weak muscle. You stop practicing and the muscle goes soft. Think of a project having a beginning, middle and end. We may through projects and practices all the time.

You may want to do this exercise with a partner. Let the partner scribe while you talk. Then switch roles.

The key to this exercise is to see yourself at the end of your life, having accomplished your lifelong goals. From this resultant vantage point, answer the following questions:

1) What was worth accomplishing in your life?
2) What were the specific qualities/traits required to achieve what you said was worth accomplishing?
3) What were the specific projects you did to accomplish what you said was worth doing? (relates to question #1).
4) What were the specific practices you did to develop/strengthen the qualities you identified in question #2?

CHAPTER THREE

# Simon Says

*Over the years I have learned that that when I don't listen to my own inner voice, my soul screams.*

*No matter what you tell yourself, there is no way to still the voice that is who you are as a human being. Your spirit finds a way to speak.*

*The soul is always speaking.*

*Do we listen?*

## *The Relationship between Vision and Time*

### *We don't live on time we live in time.*
### African Proverb

Dreaming and bringing to life one's dream, whether we're young or old requires a commitment of time. Ironically, the identity we have given Time has us feel estranged from ourselves. We are constantly haggling with Time as if it is a person who wants more than we can give. We either have too much or too little time to pursue our dreams. In our organizations, Time has become an enemy we compete against for our survival. Time has become the intruder from whom we protect ourselves. "It's only a matter of time", we tell ourselves before something good or bad occurs. Time has taken on mammoth proportions---becoming a monster whose presence evokes fear and distrust.

Sometimes we try to outwit time by covering our tracks, or taking different routes to reach our goal, or trying to buy time for ourselves. For a moment we actually believe we are one step ahead of this mysterious creature, which wears many faces, whose presence either delights or defeats us.

Early in the coaching relationship my clients lament the amount of time they have given to their careers, which has emptied them of passion, joy or hope. "We cannot leave our positions to go do what we love in life. We want to live differently, we want to contribute, but that would mean a loss of all that we have accomplished here--all that we have earned in time and money". Trapped by their thinking, they become paralyzed, afraid they cannot create something new. They wait for something external to change the direction they're taking, like new management introducing new policies, or being moved from one position to another as part of a restructuring effort. They bemoan their fates while they play solitaire on their computers. "It's only a matter of time before we retire," they tell themselves. Time continues whether we act or not.

When we are diagnosed with life threatening diseases Time becomes a militant soldier whose commands we obey because we feel indebted or trapped in its clutches. We try to buy whatever time we can by negotiating with doctors, families, and god. Rather than learn how to enjoy the passage of time as James Taylor sings in "Secret O' Life," we fight Time as if it is our enemy.

I have found Time stands still when I kiss, but it does not stop. Our past, present and future merge in a kiss. We breathe in each other's goodness. We break away but our whole being longs to hold onto the experience. What choice do we have in this moment? We can try to hold onto something already fleeting, or we can lean over to touch our lips again. Life continues as we ponder what to do next. We pray that the next kiss will be as joyful as the last. As our lips touch our hearts beat, our minds pause, the breath merges. This is living in time.

### How Does Time Relate To The Visioning Process?

Those of us who resent or are frustrated by our inability to make things happen fast enough will be frustrated by our incompetence to quickly figure out our vision. We may be experts in lots of areas, but many of us are beginners in the visioning process. By giving yourself permission to be slow, or even uncoordinated in the process, you are giving the mind time off. I have learned the hard way that it's essential to nourish ourselves so that we can quiet ourselves to hear our inner wisdom.

Farmers had it right when they planted alfalfa or any nutrient rich crop as a way to nurture and preserve their fields. We are so demanding of ourselves to get it right that we neglect replenishing ourselves in order to sustain. Letting the seeds sprout requires patience and trust. Visioning is not something that works automatically because you tell yourself you have two days to complete the process. Sometimes you can force the action, but visioning takes the time it takes.

Whatever transition we experience Time becomes an integral

ingredient in the process. Can we live in an open and honest relationship with time? Each breath we take gives us another moment of life. Can we learn to respect and honor our relationship to time? Can we slow ourselves down to notice our breath? As we slow down we will notice life.

## Coaching:

**Instructions:** Belly buster exercise.

- Follow or observe your breath going in and out of your belly or your mouth. When your mind starts to wander or think, acknowledge the thought and bring yourself back to your breath.
- When you're snagged by an emotion or a bodily sensation acknowledge the sensation or the emotion, then bring yourself back to watching your breath.
- Do this exercise for ten minutes each day.
- You will start enjoying the peace and quiet sitting brings. You will extend your sitting time (over time).

*The Good News and Bad News about the Visioning Process:*

*"Men are not free when they are doing just what they like. Men are only free when they are doing what the deepest self likes. And there is getting down to the deepest self! It takes some diving."*

D.H. Lawrence

Once I began the reinvention process, I panicked. I was face to face with all the goodness I brought to life. Immediately, I tried to disavow all knowledge of this person. I tried to turn down the volume of my own voice. I would argue endlessly about why the person I had uncovered could not possibly be me. A phantom, or a dream, I insisted. Rather than accept and start wearing this new identity, I kept searching for ways to get rid of this person. If my vision in life was to help other people bring their visions to life, then I must care about people and what happens to them. "Yes," I told myself this part is true. "Well then," my coaches would argue, "Don't you care what happens to you?"

I realized that you couldn't bring joy to others until you bring joy to yourself. I faced the truth that what I stood for in life has goodness and mercy to it; that it was up to me to begin living in ways that were consistent with what I stood for. Not just for one day, but every day. Oh, I told myself, this smells of work. Immediately I began searching for an easy way out of self- exploration.

**What is the good and bad news about the Visioning process?**

1. The process takes resources, including time, money and people.
2. You get to see both positive and negative traits.
3. Your spirit is pure no matter how many sins you have committed.
4. It takes courage to look within.
5. The more you uncover yourself to yourself, the more you see.
6. The more you wake up to who you are or who you wish to be in life, the sadder you might feel about the many years you slept at the wheel of your life.
7. You may be asleep in life, but you are not dead.
8. A teacher always shows up to guide you.

## *Creating Your Vision: The Power of Listening*

Vision is that which we think and feel, then bring to life. But how do we quiet ourselves to think or even listen to what our wisdom communicates? How can we see the signs when we're so busy working, living, and trying to cajole Time to work for us? Listening becomes a luxury. From time to time we treat ourselves to luxuries. A vision may take form in my mind, but it doesn't just happen from thinking.

In my coaching classes, I provide a variety of exercises that will quiet the mind. I remind class participants that our minds are like mainframe computers that never shut down. By first acknowledging the messages our minds are continually sending and then bringing our attention or awareness back to the present moment, we have a chance to actually detach ourselves from the endless chatter in the background. With practice, we can discern the chatter as distinct from a kernel of truth.

We know what it feels like to meet chatter with chatter. For example, in our endless meetings, we sit together, exchange some profundities, and then zone out. Every few minutes or even seconds, we check back into the conversation to see what's been said. We tell ourselves that we "already know" what someone is going to say, so we give ourselves permission to think about more pressing matters. Or we tell ourselves, that " there is nothing we can do" so we half listen to the person's concern, offer a few perfunctory statements, stand up, shake hands and move onto the next conversation. We believe listening with any depth is a privilege that we monitor closely.

Most coaching clients admit that few people are allowed in the inner sanctum of their thinking. We cannot let the world in because we will be too vulnerable. By keeping ourselves shrouded in chatter we somehow remain removed or aloof or invulnerable to what is happening in front of us, right now. We rationalize our actions with such excuses, as we can't really listen in depth because we either don't have time, or we can't help the person, or worse, we've heard this all before. It's as if some form of us appears in conversation but the whole of us is saved for those lucky few folks we trust. We don't even realize we've disconnected in the conversation. We believe that we are doing our best to build relationships. We pray that whatever we have shared will do the trick, and then we move on. NEXT!

I don't think we are bad because we half listen. Rather I think of myself as sloppy, unavailable, inauthentic, or isolated. Listening with an intention to hear not just what people say, but what they infer, suggest, hint or withhold—requires discipline and compassion. If my intention is to establish a connection then I bring my whole being to the conversation, not just my physical body. I listen with my head and heart. I'm excited to be in the conversation, willing to wait or sit with the person even when I think nothing is happening. This combined tension allows me to find the thread in what others are saying that they may not see or hear. I am present in the conversation, which means I focus my attention and awareness on the person who is speaking.

I keep my focus on what is happening in front of me no matter how intriguing the chatter in my brain. Interestingly enough, the more focused a listener I become the more effective my interactions become. People trust me and reveal their innermost thoughts or feelings. The best part is I feel really alive.

The visioning process is great training ground for listening. The more barriers you remove from the listening environment, the more you hear a whole person speaking, whether that person is you or someone else.

Monitoring how you listen is a good first step. As I said earlier the mind is a great entertainment center, with a variety of channels operating at the same time. I think of my brain chatter like a soap opera, constantly running, with little change from day to day. I love the characters I portray. Sometimes, I am glued to the seat of my own soap opera, deeply entrenched in my own story. Of course my story is always right. Imagine sitting in a room where many folks are glued to the screen of their own stories. I keep practicing quieting my brain chatter so that I can hear myself think. Most of us don't even realize how prevalent the programming is in our day-to-day existence until we begin disengaging from our stories. Meditation is a powerful practice, guiding us to become better observers of our thoughts. Over time, by practicing sitting mediation, we begin to experience some separation from our routine programming to hear more deeply, more kindly, and with greater intuition. Here is a simple exercise to quiet the mind.

## Coaching Exercise: Listening

**Instructions:**
Next time you are in a meeting, or talking with someone notice how often your mind makes judgments, or starts wandering into different topics. If you can make notes identifying the comments your mind makes do it. You will be amazed how preoccupied your mind is with other things other than the person in front of you.

<u>Sample Comments include</u>:

I already know this.
Why am I here?
I am hungry, thirsty, and angry.
I can read this later
I could do this better. This sucks. What's the point? Etc. etc.

1. Once you get used to the mind wandering off,
2. Acknowledge or thank the mind for sharing. Say Thanks.
3. Breathe deeply.
4. Bring yourself back to the meeting or conversation.

## The Honorable Moody Tidwell, Retired Judge U.S. Federal Claims Court

"When I'm sitting on the bench, I practice totally listening, focusing my attention on totally listening. I think that kind of listening begins an hour before I go on the bench. I know that I'm going to be listening to two lawyers argue a strange set of circumstances, who try to tell me what their opinion means.

When witnesses are talking, I have to use my listening totally, not only to hear what they are saying, but how they are saying it. I have to determine the truthfulness of testimony. I don't have a jury to fall back on. I am the sole trier of fact and law. I listen to their body language, their delivery, their tone and their logic. And it's not a skill. It can be a sixth sense that ability to put yourself into a space to listen. It is an honesty and openness or stance that a human being takes and then you keep looking at your actions to see if in fact that stance you're taking shows up in your actions. In many ways, I have to give lawyers the space to be brilliant. It's like swinging a golf club. When you hit it right, it's just smooth and there is whack and the ball goes like a bat out of hell. When you hit it wrong, it clunks and dribbles.

When you've go to trial with two really sharp lawyers, it's beautiful. When you go into one where they are not that way, with either inexperience or lack of integrity, honesty, whatever it is, it's like the ball dribbling and clunking. It becomes much more difficult to decide the case because you are not getting the information you need. You are also a little bit more suspect of what you are hearing because you wonder, " Are they being inept or are they trying to hide something?"

### The Visioning Process

The visioning process frees us to expand how we see ourselves, what we expect of ourselves, even what we assume to be right, true or acceptable. Our job is to free ourselves to be happy. Many of us shy away from self- exploration because it feels too touchy feely or worse, we may find something in the process that truly scares us. Our worse fears will be realized as we scrape away the layers of our own narrative. Whatever our rationale for by- passing self-exploration, I have found that the spirit always finds a way through the cracks. By participating fully in a visioning process we come face to face with all that we love and hold dear, all that we pray for and are afraid to ask, all that we need or want. Well, maybe not today, maybe after the kids finish college.

Reinvention requires opening up the self to see what is underneath. Whether demons pop out, old ghosts or memories of great loves lost, it matters little because reinvention is the opportunity to create a new identity; one that more closely aligns with the person we wish to be.

Visioning is like daydreaming; something as kids we did with great enthusiasm and gusto. Whether we stayed up all night fabricating wild tales with our friends, or simply lay in the tall grasses letting our minds wander as clouds meandered across the sky, we were very comfortable dreaming great dreams. Our fantasies helped us explore, explain, justify events and feelings that confounded or pained, scared or excited us. No matter where we grew up, day dreaming and sharing our dreams was a way of explaining life and our relationships. We invented ways to live and survive, to set ourselves free from all that constrained us. How do we create that sense of abandon now? Are you willing to play in the tall grasses again?

## Practice:
## Back To Basics: 10-Minute Day Dreaming

**Instructions:**

Why not approach visioning the same way you approach creating a gourmet dinner or baking a cake. Cooking requires specific ingredients used in specific ways that over time yield specific results. Most important to any chef or baker is the desire to create something out of nothing. Think like a chef.

**Ingredients Needed:**
Old magazines. Scissors. Glue. Poster board or construction paper. Tabletop.

Preparation:

- Choose one area of your life you would like to enhance.
- Go through the magazines and cut out pictures and words that describe the enhancements you would like to see.
- Once you cut out pictures, arrange them like a collage on the construction paper. Glue the pictures.
- You can use words and pictures to illustrate your vision.
- Hang up your collage somewhere you can see it.

If your mind is preoccupied with a thousand errands or details, you may want to quiet yourself first before you tackle a visioning exercise. What are some relaxing exercises you can do? There is no generic way to quiet the mind. Each person has his/her own stress reduction activities that work from doing an hour of yoga, to taking a bath, from getting a massage to brushing the cat. Whatever works for you, do it.

## Coaching:
## **Relaxation Exercises:**

Close your eyes and do deep breathing for five minutes.
If your mind wanders, why not listen to a relaxation tape.

　Finger paint or do water colors for thirty minutes.

　Doodle while you listen to some great jazz or classical music.

　Read your favorite poems aloud.

Meditate. Write a poem. Rock in a rocking chair.

Do nothing at all. Zero. ZIP. Nada. And stay awake.

Give yourself permission to dream. There is no right or wrong way to visioning. You will know when you have tapped into your inner wisdom. Dreaming about what is possible in your life is not a one shot deal. Some of us become so well habituated to our current lives that we need many day dreaming exercises before we find the gems.

Here are some conditions to foster daydreaming:
- Make as big a mess as you need to dream big.
- Note to yourself and others that you will clean up after yourself.
- Be willing to stick your fingers in your own vision to see if appeals to your taste buds.

## Dr. Richard Barnett, National Basketball Association, Retired.

*"Most athletes know the end is near. It's always near but they try to block it out psychologically and emotionally because the other side is something they don't want to deal with. Most of them are not qualified to go on and do anything else at that particular time. You've got to plan for the end. You have got to have a structured plan. How do I move from one discipline to another? The problem is the beginning and the end of a career should intersect with a new beginning. As you come to the end, you should be ready to take off. Most players come to the end and there is nothing on the other side. 'Where do you go from here? Who are you? What is your purpose for living?' are the questions players need to ask themselves while they are still playing."*

# Section Two: Structures

CHAPTER FOUR

# Let's Pretend

*Are you going to work for your life or work for your job?*

> Huey Richardson National Football League

*If you want to get to heaven, you've got to find a way to get there.*

**Old Cowboy Line**

*Structures help us translate vision into action.*

When I was sixteen I used Weight Watchers as the structure to support my dream of being svelte. Although I tried to lose weight on my own, I found that by attending weekly meetings, following a series of guidelines that included weighing my food portions, I was able to lose the extra weight.

I was embarrassed about being weighed in and scared to have my "weakness" revealed in front of others, but I was also tired of listening to myself complain about my looks. When you are an overweight teenager, the world weighs heavily on your emotions. By putting a structure around my dream of being thin, I was able to achieve my goal.

I am not saying that the Weight Watchers program works for everyone; what I am suggesting is that we all need a structure that supports the visioning process. How do I get from here to there?

The Weight Watcher system also provided various emotional connections I needed to stay the course. I was not fighting myself. I was teaming with a room full of other people who shared a similar vision. We all wanted to see ourselves differently. The structure included both visible and invisible components enabling us to achieve our goals. Some weeks we won because we lost a pound or two, other weeks we lost. Yet every time we gathered around the scale we laughed. Our focus shifted from our stories about what we could _not_ do or could _not_ eat to how we were playing the game at home with our families, in the world with our friends. The more we practiced with the Weight Watcher guidelines, the better we played. I began to trust the weight loss coaches, and looked forward to sharing my ups and downs with others. Everyone in the room wanted to live their lives differently, to reinvent themselves into slim, healthy people.

The Weight Watchers program alone is not the answer because structure alone does not bring about a vision. However, for many people, weight loss structures provide essential support.

Over time what this structure facilitated was a change in how I viewed myself. The structure enabled me to listen with more kindness to my own stories about success and failure in the area of weight loss/gain. I learned how to be kinder to others, because I began noticing the similarities in our stories. None of us were perfect. The weight loss structure allowed us to find a way to our own piece of heaven. By removing many of the pressures we applied to ourselves, we were better able to play the weight loss game to win.

Structures provide support, shelter, guidance, regulation, consistency, balance, space, and information. Structures can serve as containers for our thoughts, spaces for our stuff, edifices that house us, backboards against which we develop our competence, systems upon which we depend for our general well being. Structures are not built in isolation nor can we live in isolation to what we have structured. Most important, structures can change as we change.

*Wanting It Is One Thing*
*Doing It Is Another*
*Being Able to Do It Is a Whole Other Thing Again!*

## Coaching Question:

Do the structures or systems you have in place support you to bring your vision to life?

We are quick to put structures in place because we believe that structures are concrete, visible and provide a modicum of stability. The structures may have little relationship to the vision, but at least they are in place. People believe that having structures in place will make everything all right.

Let's look for a moment to the person who flies by the seat of his pants with few if any systems in place. Several years ago I was working with a very talented and technically competent woman who had been promoted to a highly visible position in her organization. In her new role, not only was she asked to publish and present technical research papers, but she also represented her organization to the media, and various public interest groups. She could talk like a technical junkie for hours, but when she began talking with "regular" people about the impact of specific issues on their lives, she was distant, and mired in details. To focus on what she was saying meant you, as the listener had to work very hard. Most people will not work that hard. We tune out, even if the information presented is valuable.

Our initial coaching sessions were held in my office. She was punctual and even excited to take on the assigned practices and projects. Over the course of two months something changed. She stopped keeping her appointments, and her assignments were incomplete. I couldn't figure out what was missing. I didn't want to change the practices I had given her because it was not a question of her inability to complete the assignments. If you just looked at my client you would assess that she had all the details of her life handled. Even in her day planner she used different highlighter pens to identify the variety of meetings, appointments, actions and results.

Sometimes coaches have to dig in the dirt to find the truffles. By quieting myself I realized that I had to go to the client's home to work with her. The best think I did was go to her. What I saw amazed me because the structure in which she lived did not support her to be coordinated, organized or focused. There was stuff everywhere. She was a hoarder.

The amount of clutter on every shelf, in every nook and cranny prevented the "real" caring person to emerge. Only the details got out. She had no system of organization in her physical work or living spaces. I asserted that she lived in a chaotic home environment that intruded on her ability to concisely articulate her thoughts.

We spent three months cleaning and recycling papers, books, bags of "household items" until there was room to move about freely. As a result of the deep cleaning, her ability to articulate more succinctly improved. She reduced an eighteen-page resume to two pages. She redid her living room to reflect the qualities of serenity she herself eschewed. The cleaning process had set her free. By revamping the organizational systems in her office we provided greater freedom for her to pursue the outcomes she wanted.

There are many examples of people who have an eye for details but have no system in place to file or organize the many details they see. In fact, they resist implementing systems that will support their work to flourish. Spontaneity is wonderful, but I have learned that you have to walk the middle of the road by balancing the need for structures as a way to create what you want and the need for spontaneity or the lack of structures as a way to free yourself to create. Balancing structures is like sitting on a see-saw. Too much or too little weight on one end brings the see-saw down. Even when you hit the marvelous balance, you must keep adjusting your position. You cannot simply hold the balance by sheer will.

In several of the federal agencies where I conduct coaching programs, I have seen how employees become divided over the implementation and use of new technological systems. People take sides fighting to retain old systems that still work rather than risk looking foolish or making mistakes trying to learn new systems. I even see this clash of old and new in my own business as I grapple with innovative ways to work with my customers. I can see the value of implementing new systems but each step is tenuous and scary because I cannot integrate in my mind the relationship between old and new.

Until I get enough practice using the new, I will keep relying on the old. But at least I have established a network of support people, from coaches to experts, who provide the backdrop yada, yada. Balance comes and goes. You're either going to be sitting on the bottom feeling weighted down by the structure or else you will be hanging in mid air. Both places offer some comfort but in the end both partners on the see-saw try to bring themselves back into balance. An easy way to tell if the structures you have in place are supporting you is to assess them. For example, if you have decided that being healthy is worth doing, you may want to look at the structures or systems you have in place that promote health. Where do you begin?

## Structure Check:

Once you have identified your vision, make a list of all the structures you have in place to bring the vision to life.

You can either go from room to room or drawer to drawer or simply sit quietly in your room reviewing what you have in place that allows you to bring what you want to life. Do not judge what you have in place good or bad. Simply observe the systems in your home or office.

## Kathy Wilson: Pro Basketball Player, Australia
## US College Basketball Coach

*"It takes courage to bridge the gap between wanting to do something and putting your words into action. I'm baffled why so many girls or women don't work towards their goals. They dream about goals, they talk about them; they just don't do the work necessary to make their goals happen. I don't want to limit their thinking, because at a certain age if you say it's not possible, they will believe you for the rest of their lives. I coach a lot of inner city girls with bad attitudes.*

*You have to be honest yet fair with teenage girls. I treat them respectfully, but I have standards; if they don't follow the rules, then I have to let them go. But I always let them know I love and care about them. I ask them what they want to be in their lives and they tell me why it's not going to happen. I tell them their dreams start today in the classroom--that it's up to them to do what it takes to make their dreams come true. Half these girls don't have any real good reason why what they want to happen-won't!*

*I know that the less prepared they are now, on and off the court, the worse off I will be later."*

## Dr. Richard Barnett, National Basketball Association, Retired

*"I think you start planning for your life when you are still playing, only it's not structured, in term of putting your hands on what you are actually gong to do. Most players think about retirement and what they're going to do, but they don't know how to get there. There is no game plan.*

*I developed a game plan but it was more a transformation. I just didn't stop playing ball one day and decide what I was going to do. It was a maturation process over a period of years. I was trying to focus on exactly what I was going to do beyond playing professional basketball. Most players don't think they are going to need additional skills additional training. They think what they're doing presently is going to sustain them over a long period of time. Nothing could be further from the truth. You've got to lay plans for your life. I lecture athletes all the time and the first question I start with is:*

*'The first contract that you signed is the beginning of the end of your career. The end is coming. Are you prepared to do something else?"*

CHAPTER FIVE

# It's a Universal Thing

*If we are willing to hear the messages our systems convey we can learn a lot about ourselves, others, what we need, and certainly what harms our growth. Structures may be built to last, but in what condition are they now?*

## Ben Nighthorse Campbell, Former Senator, Colorado

*"Pueblo Indians had three basic tenets. One of them was a strong belief in their religion. They believed everything was related, arts, religion, all one. You were a subject of a greater force that was seeing and watching you. Second, they had a very strong family unit, an extended family; everyone in the family took care of you and everybody within that family structure, even the clan leaders tried to teach and nurture each person. No such thing as abandonment, incest or abuse of children. Third, they had a strong belief that they were a part of Mother Earth. Whatever they did to earth they did to themselves.*

*Even though they may have burnt the grass on the prairie to make fresh grass come up, they almost never did anything that would cause desecration to the earth. Yes, they did limited mining but they mined with great reverence. They did things out of necessity, but they prayed for it, and they used all that they took. These three tenets kept them strong and centered. For me, as a public servant, I have to keep asking myself. How do I make fundamental change to make a better society?"*

When I began this book I related my story about Trixie and the demise of our friendship, a structure upon which I had depended for many years. One of the things I noticed as I went through the transition was how I had fallen into my relationship with Trixie. Not that we continuously built a relationship but neither did we (Trixie and I) ever review the condition of our friendship. We assumed we would always be just like we were. I began reviewing what friendship meant to me and for me. Not only was I reinventing my relationship to myself, I was also redesigning my relationships with my friends.

Questions I asked myself included:
1. What did I want in a friendship?
2. What qualities did I value in others?
3. What qualities did I value in myself that I could bring to my friendships?
4. What were my needs from a friend?

**5.** What was I willing to do and not to do to build a friendship?

**6.** How would I know if a friendship was "right" for me?

Mulling over these questions helped me shape my own needs, expectations and goals around friendship.

## Coaching:
## Law of the 7th Generation: Connecting Vision to Action

What connects Vision and Structure is planning. Senator Ben Nighthorse Campbell pointed out the Law of the 7th Generation used by Native American Indians is an effective way to determine what is worth doing in the short and long run. Identifying and analyzing the impact of one's choices on the next seven generations is essential in any tribal decision making process. If you balk when thinking seven generations, then simply create some arbitrary timetables you can review (3, 5 or 10 years).

As I weave a network of friends my intention is to stay mindful of the quality of relationship I am cultivating. By sifting through my relationships, I transformed them in some ways, adding ingredients as needed, removing some ingredients that were not helpful to either party. Generally I am a lot more attentive to people, noticing their joys and their pain, which gives me greater joy and sadness too.

By not taking my friendships for granted, I am infusing them with new life. I keep my intention of how I want to be with my friends in the forefront of my thinking. With clarity around my intention, I can easily monitor and correct my actions along the way. Are my actions consistent with my intention? What is your intention in your relationships? What outcomes are you seeking for yourself as you put your time, energy and heart into these relationships? What kinds of systems have you implemented that will support your relationships to flourish?

As you keep peeling the layers of your life to see what is underneath, you will find old relics, trash and small gems in need of polishing. Without attaching blame to why something is in its current condition, why not invite yourself to stand in the question. Begin an inquiry into an area of your life.

The following questions will stimulate your thinking:
1. How does your current structure(s) support you to bring your vision to life?
2. What do you wish to keep of this current structure?
3. What adjustments, if any, do you need to make so that your structures support you?
4. How will making these adjustments assist you?
5. What do you have to give up or let go of in order to move forward?
6. What will it take in terms of resources, time, energy, people or money to make the systems changes you are talking about?
7. How do you need to be or what specific traits do you need to realize your goals?
8. What are the short and long-term consequences (positive and negative) you anticipate if you make the desired changes?
9. What could go wrong? How can you overcome the obstacles in your path?

CHAPTER SIX

# The House that Jack Built

*You can't buy the change you want, you have to grow it.*

*Dr. Frederic Hudson*

The slogan "Built to last" conveys a powerful message of longevity, reliability, and stability. These features are valuable if and when they meet a specific need. However, these features contradict the progress of man's mind when applied to all parts of our human existence. The system's job is to work for the individual or organization. When we listen with an intention to hear, we will learn the messages our systems reveal. Over the past two decades I have coached many great professionals who micro manage their employees. Managers complain about having no time to do their jobs as identified in their job description. Employees complain that they lack autonomy to take projects from start to finish. Everyone complains about the lack of trust in the organization. Everyone wants something to change but they have grown accustomed to their particular way of doing business. In many ways they are frozen in their management patterns.

By finding ways to help them reframe their problems so that they can see options, they are freer to re-design their management habits. Over time, a system —even one that produces regular breakdowns— becomes part of how people do business. Rather than review the impact of the system on people, we develop coping mechanisms that allow us to survive within the system. The irony of the "Built To Last" slogan is that nothing lasts.

In many of the organizations where I coach, management knows something is off. They would like to see improvements, they'd like to spend less time shielding one person from another, listening to endless tales of woe or even lamenting the amount of time they waste listening to stories that do not have happy endings, but if the improvements require confronting people, or holding folks accountable for their actions it is often easier to simply turn the other cheek and walk away.

We keep repairing broken systems in the hope that the patch jobs will work. And for some period of time, patch jobs work. Sometimes consultants are called in. But often managers choose to not follow the recommendations. People may go to training but the new skills learned in the training room fall to wayside in an environment that neither supports innovation nor advocates for its employees. People may bounce back from crisis in the organization, but over time these same people lose their spirit to create, to innovate, or to lead.

It's not that my clients are good or bad people, rather they have learned to tune out or filter out the creaks and groans of their systems. Sometimes their listening is like a cul de sac in the road, where words and pictures enter, circle around a neighborhood of thoughts, then leave the same way they entered. Nothing stays. My job is to wake people up to become better observers of their own performance within the systems they have built. As my clients begin seeing more clearly how they think, speak and act, they are more open to co-creating practices that will help them re-frame issues in new or improved ways.

How do you know when it's time to reinvent your system? The easiest way to tell if your system provides the results you declare are worth having is by monitoring your system in action. Does the structure support you and your employees to achieve or does the system work against what the organization stands for? If you cannot identify a system in your life to observe why not try the following exercise as guide?

## Instructions:

Write down everything you do in a ONE-DAY period.
Include when you do things, where, with whom, how you get things done and why you do things the way you do.

*Do this exercise for five days.* At the end of five days, begin grouping similar activities under one heading i.e. Personal Calls covers all individual calls you make. After you have grouped individual activities into single headings, begin noticing the patterns that emerge. What do these patterns tell you about how you live?

You may want to pull your hair out after tracking your activities for five days, but you will definitely have the information you need to start observing what systems if any you have in place.

## Bruce Lehman, Commissioner (former) U.S Patent and Trademark Office

*"Fear inevitably leads to destructive and self-destructive activity. Prudence has an element of recognizing fear. But people who are fundamentally afraid will not reinvent anything. They will never accomplish anything. Since the society in which we live changes in ways that absolutely require an adjustment in all kinds of things, the fear, which prevents you from adjusting, will ultimately be destructive."*

## Gordon Graham, Ex- Convict, CEO of Graham and Associates, Inc.

*"You have to develop a frame of reference if you are truly going to reinvent yourself. You have to go back, change and evaluate some of the things that used to be the truth but are no longer relevant. We operate automatically on a lot of information that is no longer relevant to who we are now, or what we want in our lives. You have to ask yourself, Where did this information come from? Who put these barriers in my thinking?"*

## *What Do YOU Need to Know About Structures?*

I believe a structure is organic, alive. If we view structures or systems as an environment we inhabit, we begin to engage differently with it. What's possible is our increased skill to discern what works or does not work within the structures we inhabit. As you begin observing the structures you may notice that how you have lived, for example, has contained you more than set you free.

As an exercise, walk through your home. Pause in each room and notice your mood as you walk from one room to the next. What happens to your mood? Is there one room where you feel most comfortable or relaxed? Ask yourself in which room of your house you feel most alive? Review your furniture, blinds, windows, and doors. Does this environment encourage family members to create and express themselves or does the construction of the rooms, the furniture in the rooms or the decor close down the doors of creativity and communication? What is the nature of the communication in your home?

Architect Frank Lloyd Wright quotes the Bible when he asserts: *"The kingdom of God is within you. That is where architecture lies. That is where humanity lies. That is our future. If we are ever going to amount to anything, it is all there now; we simply have to develop it. That is what I call human nature or humanity."*

As I get older I realize that for all the good a system or structure provides, it is neither impenetrable nor permanent, no matter how well it has been constructed. In fact, the harder we hold onto the systems we have created, the less likely we are to see how the system may actually be working against us. Not only do we need to review the quality or condition of our structures, we also want to review current structures for how well they support us to keep evolving in our thinking.

*"I am not an advocate for frequent changes in laws and constitution, but laws and institutions must go hand in hand with the progress of the human mind. As that becomes more developed, more enlightened and new discoveries are made, new truths discovered, and manners of and opinions change, with the change in circumstance, institutions must advance also to keep pace with these times."*
**Thomas Jefferson**

Walking through the homes designed and built by Frank Lloyd Wright, I felt the world outside merging with the world he had created inside. His designs allowed the world outside the concrete house walls to interact with nature. Wright created ways for us to remember and celebrate trees, animals and water. What does a Frank Lloyd Wright home have to do with a conversation about structures? His homes give us a sense of lightness that results in our increased ability to interact with our thoughts and feelings, as well as interact with greater ease with nature. What happens for you in your home or office?

Whether we are talking about the structure of your home, the structure of your life, or the business systems you have in your organization, the bottom line question is "Tell me how your structures promote openness to learning and to living?" Why not begin observing the impact of your structures on your spirit, performance, mood, relationships, etc.?

Let's revisit the micro manager and his staff. The prevalent mood in his organization is frustration. There is a lack of trust between co-leaders. Work gets done but they battle constantly among themselves. A lot of time is wasted not following through on project action plans because employees have not developed fundamental business systems upon which each person can rely. Yes, they do have systems, but current systems do not relate to the vision of their business.

Although they are talented and skillful they are constantly frustrated in their efforts to complete their jobs. Not a good work environment. Creativity, spontaneity, joy seem to be missing. Employees are focusing their "limited" energy to fix those parts of the organization where they feel most comfortable. No new ideas or innovations have emerged in several years.

As part of their coaching program I am helping managers and staff define and establish a vision from which they can review their current business systems. Although they took a year to finally commit to working with a coach, in the first two month they made remarkable progress defining what is worth doing in their business and evaluating their current business policies.

For those of you who are looking to win again in life, reinventing your systems might appear quite threatening, if not downright impossible. When we are faced with taking down or taking apart that which we have known and relied upon, we want to pull the shades down on our thinking; wait out the changes. I don't believe you can wait out the changes. Even those of us who sit on the bench of life get frustrated.

*"We meet ourselves time and time again in a thousand disguises on the path of life."*

Carl Jung, Psychologist

### *Structures Communicate*

Reinvention is the process of finding and acquainting yourself with the many different "selves" you have, and learning how to integrate these independent selves into one whole human being. Maintaining our integrity is the result of integrating the various aspects of the self. If we cannot or will not listen to our inner voices or bodies when they speak to us, how can we listen to the voices of others who are in similar discomfort or pain?

As you begin investigating your systems, you get to communicate with the messages your systems convey. Listening with an intention to hear, speaking with an intention to connect with yourself or another human being, reading with an intention to educate yourself about yourself, and finally, writing with an intention to hear yourself speak. Based upon this communication you will be able to design actions that support reinvention.

When coaching, I focus myself to listen to the impact of the message a structure communicates—not the message itself. Many clients feel that the structures in place are valuable because they are new, or expensive or state of the art. However, it is not the system itself that I watch. Rather I pay attention to how the implementation of the system affects the individuals or the organization. Do the systems help people achieve their desired outcomes? If they do, great, if they don't, why not? My colleagues maintain that coaches sniff for truffles. I encourage my clients to sniff for truffles as well. How can they sniff? Through reading, writing, speaking and listening to the messages being communicated as they interact with systems.

For example, I have suggested that an internal Public Information Organization review the value and benefits of its various communication tools. At first they were hesitant, because in their opinion, they had a variety of tools that worked. "But how do you know they address your customers' needs?" I wanted to know. "What questions do your customers have? And do your communication vehicles answer these questions?" My prodding resulted in the team developing a survey questionnaire for users. The responses helped them re-frame the context and content of their communication tools to better serve their customers.

## Richard Goodstein, Advanced Certified Rolfer

*"The body has a natural wisdom-- it knows when it works and doesn't work. When you listen, you'll feel it and you'll know it's okay. And if you don't listen, something is going to happen and it's going to tell you that something is wrong. Bodies get information. Most people override it, not listening to the messages. But there is integrity to the system. We don't pay attention because we are living in a world that goes way too fast. Most people look at their body like it's a given, but that's not true. The Body is a creation.*

*When I work on your body, I am not simply working on a structure; I am working on a person. There is an enormous spirit in that person. What that spirit is about has a lot to do with the kind of changes that are going to go on during the Rolfing sessions. There is no separation between the mind and the body."*

## Kathy Wilson, Pro Woman's Basketball Player, Australia Coaches College Basketball (Women)

*"Prepare yourself for survival by having a "Never Give up Attitude". When one thing doesn't work in sports, you have to try something different. If this offense isn't working, change it and try something else. In life, it's the same thinking. Just because the system you have in place isn't working, doesn't mean it's not a good idea. It may simply mean you have to change the way you are doing it. Change your strategy. Change your offense and try again. Not only trying a different strategy but also be willing to try harder."*

### *Structures Provide Feedback and Healing*

When I view my own body as a mainframe computer with my brain serving as the command center, I realize that each major system in my body is in regular ongoing communication with the brain. Even when we have convinced ourselves that we understand how the body works physically, it seems our understanding and knowledge still cannot provide cures for the many devastating diseases in our society. Rather than arrogantly insist that I understand or know how things work, or blatantly ignore the relationship between systems, I am learning to simply observe how one system affects the overall operation. Why not begin watching your own body in action? Or observe your moods. Is there a physical symptom expressed by your body when you are trapped in a negative mood?

Sometimes the physical symptoms are a better indicator to what your mood is than anything your mind tells you. Learning to read and listen to your body will give you good insight into your mental state. Your dialogues about system enhancements or breakdowns can be directed to your body, your home, or work environment-- any structure upon which you rely. There are two keys to keep in mind as you engage with structural renewal.

1. Keep your eyes open and look.
2. Practice kindness with yourself no matter what you find.

## Practice:
## Mind and Body System Exercise: Five to Ten Minutes

**Instructions:**
You want to discover how your mind and body relates. Take a five or ten minute break. Close the door. Sit quietly or lie down on the floor. Close your eyes. Inhale/ exhale three times slowly.

- Bring your attention to your body. Move your focus to your head. Scan your head and face with your eyes closed. Notice any sensations, pains or stresses in your head and face. Focus on where the sensation is. Ask yourself: What is your body telling you right now? What does your body need?

- Breathe deeply listening with closed eyes to your body's messages.
- Do this scanning exercise for each major part of your body, including your chest, arms, legs, hands, abdomen, and genital area. Etc. When you have completed the scan, breathe deeply again.
- Acknowledge your body for supporting you in life.

Open your eyes.

CHAPTER SEVEN

# Let's Play Doctor

## Richard Goodstein, Advanced Certified Rolfer

*"My clients tell me that they have to be at work at a certain time; they can't take time off during the day to take care of themselves because there is a fear that someone is trying to cheat the company. That's not healthy. If you give people an opportunity to move around and breathe, they are going to be more productive. Their brains are going to work a whole lot better. The brain gets stimulated by diversity and movement. I teach my clients to recognize that everything they think and feel, that their body is doing the same thing.*

*Who is going to take the risk--who is going to take the leap and say, "This is what I value. This is what is going to make life work better?" I'm running into more and more people who are incredibly stressed out. They don't have a clue what breathing looks like. They are gasping for air. That's not healthy. I don't think there is enough understanding of the human body. There is not enough respect for what it means.*

*Structural awareness means asking, what would it look like if it was working or healthy?"*

Often we concentrate our efforts on maintaining, rebuilding, or developing systems that we can see, touch or feel. By concentrating our resources (time, money or people) insuring that these structures work efficiently, we believe we are re-inventing our lives or our businesses. Our focus on one element (structures) to the exclusion of others shields or distracts us from reviewing how well our intentions match up with our results. By convincing ourselves that the systems we have built although not perfect are better than nothing, we give ourselves more time to suffer. In time, we secretly tell ourselves, we will eliminate nagging problems.

Reinvention requires suspending our beliefs about how we think our business or lives "ought" to run. Several years ago I was worked for a manager director who was told by his executive director to restructure his department into teams. In order for this staff to even begin the work of reorganizing themselves, we first spent several weeks grappling with the following questions:

## Coaching Exercise: Let's Play Doctor

**Instructions:** Ask yourself the following questions in relationship to reinventing a particular system or structure. Customize as appropriate.

1. What do I/we need to do and for whom do we do it?
2. How well do we currently do what we do?
3. What do we need to improve, alter or change?
4. What are some of the outcomes of these changes?
5. How will these changes impact our relationships at work and at home?
6. How can we best structure these changes so that they are made with the least amount of down time?
7. How will we know when the changes we have made meet our needs and our goals?

By addressing these questions in a sincere and open forum, employees actually tapped into their vision of the department. They noticed that in their efforts to complete their day- to- day operations, which included, identifying and completing projects accurately and on time, they had somehow lost touch with their customers. They may have been doing lots of projects, but they realized that their work time would be more effective if they communicated and worked alongside their customers. As my dad used to say, "You're working hard not smart."

As the staff became better observers of their performance, they moved quickly into teams that supported the vision they had established. They were able to hold the vision up to scrutiny. Restructuring themselves was the first step, learning how to build and develop their teamwork approaches took longer. But over time they have continued to sharpen their tools so that their products reflect the relationship between customer and service provider. And they have learned not to take themselves quite so seriously.

## Reverend Carole Crumbley- Former Education Director Washington National Cathedral, Now at Shambala Institute

*"I think the church has a responsibility to address the question, 'what is our vision? What is our vision of the world?'. We need to ask if what we are doing relates to our vision. We say we are a house of prayer for all people, a church for national purposes yet I think we need to ask if our processes really serve that vision. I don't think we do. I think we have a church. That church has a structure; it has tools, resources, but I don't think we are connected with the vision. I think we have a fear of relinquishing control. I think churches can lead the way for people to be in relationship to spirit, but we would have to have a deepening of trust. The life of the spirit is not something you can control."*

### *Feedback and Healing, What Do They Have in Common?*

Our systems are an extension of how we bring our desires to life. If I view my body as the original mainframe, then each of the independent systems are networked in a fairly sophisticated yet simple way. Sophisticated, because even the most intelligent doctors cannot find cures for the common cold. What seems complicated on the inside responds in marvelously simple ways on the outside. What came naturally for me, like walking, was practically impossible for my handicapped mother. For each action she took, from getting out of bed in the morning to climbing up the stairs, she had to think and then act. She would bring her attention to her physical actions. And even then, her body might not comply.

Although I may not be able to diagnose the nature of this feedback, I realize that my own body constantly listens to the messages it receives from my brain. More important, my brain has developed specific habits, patterns of movement and thought that are manifested physically. There is repetition and innovation in my own system. How I learn to reinvent my own body is dependent on my willingness to listen to the messages my body communicates. I must quiet my mind to hear what is being said. Is there a particular bodily sensation worth noting, or a specific pain somewhere in my body? Is my brain in overdrive?

Based on the feedback I receive I will make a decision about what action I need to take that will bring me into alignment with what I say is worth doing or what I said is worth having. If your vision includes good health, then you will find ways to keep monitoring and correcting your actions to support wellness.

I have a good friend who has been overweight his adult life. He decided to create wellness and good health for himself. This time around, what was different in the weight loss game was he shifted his thinking from following a diet to paying better attention to the triggers in his mind. When the waters of life are calm it's easy to remember why you're doing what you do; the real test is when you can hold to your vision in the middle of a storm. My friend noticed that most of his eating was emotionally tied. Upsets with his family, lack of acknowledgement at his job, money issues, etc., all contributed to a derailment from his vision.

Over time, and with practice he has successfully learned to live with the varied emotional triggers as well as his own relationship to various issues. He has learned that his emotions regarding varied issues come and go so that he no longer has to react with binging to quell the storms brewing in his mind. The volume of self-destructive conversations has diminished. Not gone away, but diminished sufficiently for him to stay on track with his desired outcomes. More important, the more time he has put into adhering to his weight loss practices, his awareness of the triggers affords him greater opportunity to pause and reframe these issues in ways that free him to take effective action. In our many conversations about the hold old habits have, we both recognize where we get trapped, and we devise better ways to avoid the traps. Someday, he hopes, he won't entrap himself with his thinking about weight because his commitment to wellness will be stronger than his attachment to the emotional triggers.

My mother never gave up her daily struggle to simply put one foot in front of the other. She got tired with this fight, but her vision was to remain in her own home, be as independent as possible. By putting several support systems in place, she fulfilled her vision.

I use the body as a discussion point for structures because it is something around which we can all relate. We all have bodies. We can view our bodies like an institution upon which we build specific customs and patterns of thought and behavior. Are the behaviors, and customs to which we have become accustomed serving us? If you are experiencing pain in your system, whether that system is your body or your organization, what is the pain trying to tell you?

### *Healing Ourselves, Healing Our Organizations*

Healing occurs as a result of the actions we take. Healing is not a one shot deal. Whether the wounds are internal or external, healing depends on the practices we do. Healing may occur, but there is no guarantee that with healing comes a cure. You have read or heard stories of people dying of cancer or Aids who commit themselves to healing their relationships even as they are dying. Why bother healing our systems, if we can't guarantee a cure?

> *"A musician must make music, an artist must paint,*
> *a poet must write,*
> *If he is to be ultimately at peace with himself,*
> *what a man can be, he must be."*
> **Abraham Maslow**

Healing yourself or healing your systems is a state of mind you engage in because you want the benefits healing brings. Standing in the storm of your own discontent as you reinvent your structures is not life threatening. You may get blown over, tossed to the ground, wet, pummeled by hail, whipped by violent winds, but at least you're fighting for the life you have declared is worth living.

A single mother with a young child has recently made the commitment to heal her relationship with her ex-husband. Both she and her ex-husband love their child, but they cannot stand to be in the same room with one another; whatever communication they have ends up heated. Although their relationship is contentious, this woman's goal is to build a bridge with her ex-husband so they can jointly raise their child. She does not doubt the father's ability to raise their child, but they cannot productively discuss parenting issues with so much old anger and resentment present.

Although she knows there is no "cure" for this relationship, she is willing to attend and pay for counseling because she believes that if she can build a bridge with her husband where they both feel safe, they will be able to share the parenting roles. It takes a lot of courage to stand in the middle of any broken relationship. It takes courage, time, money and support from experts and loved ones to reinvent the system you have invested in and built.

## Reverend Carole Crumbley- Former Director of Education, Washington National Cathedral, Now Shambala Institute

*"In Church we teach people a love of god, but we really don't deal with the whole self. We let that happen in other places. We are concerned about maintaining the structures of the church, the buildings, the committees, paying the utilities, and if that is what building a community is all about, it doesn't do a lot for strengthening the spirit. The spirit is going to break down those edifices. I see my work as bridgework because people have always worked in the vineyard of the spirit, through body, voice, and writing, independently of churches.*

*I think our work is through the work of the spirit nurturing and supporting people to prepare them for leadership, in the church or in their faith communities. The life of the spirit is going to live. It will always find its way. Either the church is going to open up to listen, because people are coming back into the church and talking about their experiences, talking about what they need.*

*If this conversation doesn't happen, the church will just die. Maybe the church needs to die in terms of its buildings and structures, in terms of its ordained leadership. If you are open to the life of the spirit, you are free enough to let all this go."*

CHAPTER EIGHT

# ABRACADABRA

*There is nothing permanent except change.*

*Heraclitus*

## Reinventing Structures: A Holistic Approach

*"You have to become your own teacher and your own disciple."*
**Krishnamurti**

Reinventing systems, business structures, your health or your body requires a "whole" approach. What do we mean by whole? You cannot invent and implement operating systems, whether personal or organizational without considering the impact on other existing systems. We may design a marvelous solution to a particular problem, but the solution only affects a small part of the problem.

My coaching client, the micromanager, in good faith installed a project management software tool for his staff. However, not everyone knew or learned how to use the tool. Worse, after someone had spent the time to enter all pertinent project information, the rest of the staff would make scheduling and service changes as requested by customers or the micromanager. Each time someone made a physical change to the project, whether during a meeting with a client or during a phone call, that updated information was supposed to be entered in the system. But people were busy, moving from project to project. No one had the time to re-enter the changes. Just to keep up with the changes, they reverted back to outlining their projects on large newsprint paper and hanging the papers in the main office—just as they had before. No one person is guilty here, but overall they did not review what it would take in terms of time and energy to use the software package.

In this organization, one of the questions they can ask before they invest in new training, consultants or software packages is "Why are we doing this? What is going to be the impact of implementing this system in our already existing system? Who is going to be responsible for operating and maintaining this new system? How will we work with each other, and with our customers to maximize the effectiveness of any new system we install?"

## Ben Nighthorse Campbell, Former Senator, Colorado

*"I think about the Law of the Seventh Generation. You should not make a decision until you try to reflect its impact on your great grandson's grandson. I try to think about this old tribal custom when I do public policy. How will my decision affect us years and years ahead of where we are now? In the American government, this practice is not common. We tend to be reactionary, not proactive. We tend to react to whatever is the crisis at the time. Indians were great believers in dreams and the dreams would often dictate the direction they would take. We don't dream much in government; we are too busy fixing late social security checks and such.*

*I think my decision making is reconciled by the fact that when I am out of office, no one is going to give a heck about where I am, but I will remember where I was, and the decisions I made and I don't want to be ashamed of them."*

## Coaching Hints: Conditioning Counts

### Instructions:

Similar to athletes we have to get ourselves into condition before we undertake the rebuilding of systems that have guided (or sheltered) us.

1. Observe your current condition.
2. Ask yourself "Am I strong enough to weather the storms reinventing might include?"
3. If you are, great!
4. If you are not, ask yourself, "What exercises can I now undertake that will get me into better condition?"
5. Once you are in good condition, you still have to keep working out.

## *Addendum: What Conditioning Exercises Can You Do?*

1. See Section One for visioning exercises.
2. Find or build a network of support—both experts in your field and people who love you. You will need to rely on both as you reinvent your systems.
3. Learn how to make effective requests for help.
4. Make requests for help from your network of support.
5. Learn the difference between working hard not smart.
6. Take time each day to play by yourself or with others. Play is not going to the gym to work out. Play is playtime. Ask a kid.
7. Be kind to yourself. Note your progress on paper. Give yourself a star when you do well.

## Bruce Lehman, Commissioner (former), US Patent and Trademark Office

*"Communication is probably the most important aspect of facilitating change. Communicating what the conditions are, what the changes need to be, or what the fears are that people have. Communication is the starting point. You need competent leaders who can effectively communicate the need for change as well as receive feedback.*

*Whenever you change you are running into uncharted waters and sometimes you make changes that prove not to be right. Like piloting a ship when the ship is off course, you have to have some mechanism for knowing what is going on. You have to consider rapidity with which you make a change.*

*If you push an organization too fast, faster than it is capable, you are going to have a breakdown. You need to have that feedback to direct. You need to constantly be regulating a speed of change and the direction of change. You can't simply develop a plan, send people off doing it and not pay attention to it for ten years. It is a constant process that is being revisited every day."*

## Rickie C. Harris, NFL, Retired

*"How you want to be in life is more important than the game, but you don't understand that point when you are in the middle of the game. You don't understand that if you are all those things you want to be it will help you win the game."*

### *Reinventing Structures: Taking It to the Streets*

The greater your openness to receive and to see, the more you will receive and see.

If you have been experimenting as you are reading, you have become more alert to the functions, appearance, value and impact of structures or systems. Maybe you have already selected a vision or a particular dream you want to fulfill. You may already have systems in place or maybe you don't have the "right" systems in place. No matter where you stand, I find using project management or life cycle management techniques takes the mystery out of reinventing structures. Project management tools can be used at any point in the reinvention process.

Whether you are starting from the beginning trying to re-define your structures, or you are midway into a project, using project management tools strengthens your effectiveness to achieve your desired outcomes. How do you correct your progress in life if you're not willing to monitor your results? You won't. You will have a generalized sense of well being or a general sense of agitation, but you won't know for sure how well you are doing in any one area if you don't look.

Reminding yourself of what it is you said is worth doing will keep you honest as you design or redesign your structure. Ironically, I find most of us rely on basic project management tools in the workplace, but we avoid using these same tools to reinvent other important aspects our lives. Why do we steer clear of redesigning our lives? I think most of us are afraid of what we will uncover.

When I'm coaching, I listen for the natural wisdom people bring to their concerns and goals. They may have an intuitive sense about what will work for them, but after years of practicing specific habits they have become distanced from their "core self" and have no pathway to get back to how they wish to be. At times my job is to create the steps they can take; at other times my job is to provide a way for them to make the distinctions themselves about what will work more effectively. Once clients have articulated the distinctions between doing Action A and Action B, they are better equipped to take on a practice that will strengthen their competence to follow through.

There are two kinds of suffering: the kind of suffering that perpetuates more suffering and the kind of suffering that ends suffering. If I am suffering and I take no action to reduce or eliminate the pain, I am perpetuating more pain.

To be successful in a reinvention process requires feedback, support and guidance. We may know what is the best for us, but we are powerless to move. Create a change environment that provides support and feedback. Make sure you have conditions in place that support you no matter what you discover. You may want to partner with a trusted friend, or work with a coach.

Overall, you have to practice kindness with yourself. Stephen Levine, noted author and lecturer, suggested we learn how to cradle ourselves, cradling both our negative and positive emotions. Would we hold our babies with disdain? Why should we hold our emotions with anything less than kindness, even the emotions we dislike? I didn't believe it was possible to love my own anger, but when I tried the exercise, I noticed my belly softened and my anger dissolved.

Often what we find as we begin tearing down our walls is sadness about how we have lived. Be kind to yourself as you uncover things about yourself. No judgments necessary. Arguing or fighting for your own limitations as a way to justify why something cannot be changed, or why conditions must remain the way they are, may throw all of us off your track for a while, but in the end your spirit screams for attention.

## Barbara Roberts—Former Governor of Oregon

*"You can't change everybody in the world. Only person you can control is you. If I can influence others by being a good role model, by being a kind of path breaker, then setting an example is a wonderful way to change any system. If you set that kind of example, it makes it easier for others to join you. If you are politically courageous and you survive in the next election, it is a lot easier to get others to join you the next time around. I recognize that everybody didn't play by my rules and everybody didn't necessarily believe what I believed or agree with my way of doing things. I don't think you can expect them to. I had people I had no respect for, but I didn't wring my hands about it. First you recognize that it exists, you change it where you can, set examples where you can and then you recognize you are not going to win them all."*

## Gordon Graham, President, Graham and Associates

*"I was an ex-convict. When you have that self-image and label it's as though from inside yourself, it's stamped on your forehead. Because of that label, you act differently. You approach a job differently. Changing that label was critical. Another insight I had was when we are out of our comfort zone; we will work to get back to where we feel we belong. So you are comfortable doing time in prison; when you get out, you don't fit. Subconsciously you will commit some act that will get you back into prison.*

*Most important, you have to move towards and become that which you think about most often. There is a constant stream of self- talk in your brain. You look at a problem and if your self- talk constantly beats you down you cannot solve the problem. If you change the self- talk, see the problem as an opportunity, change your approach, you will begin to talk differently. Gradually, you will come to the table with energy, enthusiasm, and the belief that you can make it happen. " I am, I can, and I choose to, I want to, I act now these are triggering tools bringing me back to focus on what I want."*

*Taking It to the Streets:*

## Conducting a Self- Assessment

What is the value of conducting an assessment? It provides "sound and current data" from which we can create a strategy. I know when we're in pain we want immediate relief. Clients come to me wanting immediate results for issues that have been gnawing at their ability to produce, be satisfied, or more effective. I am constantly reminding them that although I can from time to time create a miracle, I'm not a magician. We're able to assist clients as they reframe issues so that they're "freed up" to achieve the desired outcomes. Coaches create a wholesome environment so clients can practice new tools, new ways of thinking, guiding them to respond with more ease, thereby reducing their chronic stress. Ultimately clients are competent to correct and monitor their own behaviors. We work ourselves out of a job.

When I worked with budget analysts in a large federal agency, we reviewed the definition of analysis as it related to their jobs. Included in our definition was the understanding of how their work related to and affected the agency's mission, goals and objectives. How well they strengthened this core skill depended on three factors: Practice analyzing (using the muscle), Focus (targeting the muscle) and Time (working the muscle).

Assessing raw data means watching yourself in specific ways so you will not only see the information, but you will be able to see patterns in your own behavior. Let's go back to my budget analysts who determined that analysis was an essential skill for any departmental employee. What distinguished a beginner analyst from an expert was how accurately the expert interpreted and translated patterns in budget spending and budget allocations. If clients were overspending year after year in specific areas, it was the job of the analyst to help the client either reduce spending, re-allocate funds more efficiently or design marketing measures that would be implemented to increase budget allocations.

What you find as you conduct your assessments is neither good nor bad. Occasionally, your findings affirm your gut feelings about why things are the way they are. Self-assessments can be done at different junctures along the reinvention path. If I have outlined specific outcomes for myself, I will assess my current state, check in midway through the process and re-assess at the end. Data is neither right nor wrong. It's how we interpret what we find that will influence the actions we take, whether that is designing a project, program or policy.

When I implemented core competencies for the analysts I kept our focus on two elements, the organizational and departmental vision(s) and what the employees had defined as their essential jobs. When we reviewed all the data around their definition of Analysis as a core competence, we discovered that although they identified working closely with their customers as a crucial need, they acknowledged their lack of customer interaction. They were aware of the spending patterns, but they were unable to determine why certain customers spent funds in certain ways. Because they didn't know their customers the analysts projected spending costs that oftentimes had no correlation to the specific program needs. Customers were unhappy with budget allocations, taking their complaints to senior leaders in the department, who then lambasted the analysts, who then withdrew to their cubbyholes to play computer solitaire. Why would an analyst want to get entangled with angry customers?

Assessments helped us uncover blind spots, wounded egos, and opportunities for correction. Since they wanted to be happy, and wanted their customers to stop complaining, they developed some communication tools they could implement that would resolve some of their questions. The assessment tool helped clarify the areas in which we needed to focus departmental efforts.

If you get stuck trying to design an exercise, why not go back to your vision section, and design a handful of questions to give yourself a baseline. Since we all agree we want to be happy, then finding creative ways to close the gaps between your vision and your current reality can be fun. We are all prone to skipping this step and moving directly to program design and implementation, hoping that if we move quickly, get the design in place, we will all feel better. Jumping into design does not guarantee the way out of suffering. Take your time when conducting a self-assessment.

## Coaching Tip: Is There a Good Time to Conduct an Assessment?

Anytime is a good TIME.

Since all projects have a beginning, middle and end, you can assess your progress anytime.

Why not take on the challenge of becoming a better observer?

### Rules For Designing and Conducting Your Self-Assessment

Approach conducting a self- assessment the same way you would approach purchasing a house or any big-ticket item.

Jump in when you feel confident about the decision you are making. Take your time. If you treat your own reinvention process with the same care and concern you apply to house ownership, you'll weather the emotional, spiritual, intellectual and physical storms easier, releasing pressure by not judging yourself as a good or bad person, no matter what you uncover.

1. Design a simple exercise with a focus on the part of your life you wish to study.
2. Be kind to yourself during the process.
3. Do the exercise regularly –observe yourself during the

day and in the evenings.
4. Set an intention about what you wish to discover.
5. If you do fact gathering daily, then once week ask yourself what you are learning by doing the practice.

## Program Design

Once you collect the data you'll want to design a program or action plan that will close the gap between what you have found and what you wish to have. There is no right or wrong way to design your action plan. Your plan will be focused, require practice and be conducted over time. Remember that unless you have to do emergency surgery on some aspect of your life, i.e. terminating an abusive relationship, most of the steps you plan can be small yet steady.

My micro manager, for instance, knows there are parts of his business that require "elective" surgery from developing internal business policies regarding customer service, as well as better defining employee roles and responsibilities. However, he is not ready to take these steps. What he is ready to do is focus his attention on the relationship between how he currently runs his business and the business results. Although he realizes he needs to develop and implement fundamental business practices for his staff, he is not ready to move forward in this domain. Pushing him to correct these situations does not seem to work. Encouraging him to address one small area at a time, always showing him the relationships between various systems motivates him sufficiently to keep taking on larger business issues. I think timing and pacing are important. As he becomes more at ease observing his habits and patterns around confronting personnel issues, he is also noticing the recurring breakdowns he ends up having because of his unwillingness to tackle these issues. A sense of urgency is developing that he can no longer avoid.

I believe most of us know what we need to do to alleviate our stresses or reduce recurring personal or work breakdowns, but we have become so knotted in our thinking that we are powerless to move forward. When you design your action plan, keep in mind the outcomes you seek. Ask yourself if the steps you are going to take will close the gap. Ask yourself what could get in the way of you doing your practices?

Sometimes closing the gap requires a change in our mental attitude. We have to see or view our situation in a new, distinct way that allows us to take action. You can almost define old and new thinking required for the future you want. Write down the conversations you will have to forward you with your action plan. Write the names of people who can and will support you in achieving your goals. If you have given yourself enough time and space to conduct an assessment, your program design will flow quite easily from one step to the next. When we lack sound and current data, or we spend our time guessing what something means, or we avoid looking because we don't want to see what is there in front of us, then what we design is flimsy and unreliable.

Be patient with yourself as you embark on this journey. Even the best-designed program can falter. Life has a way of creating detours just when you thought you knew where you were heading. Up front planning and preparation for obstacles will facilitate our competence to move through obstacles quickly. However, there are no guarantees we will succeed. The better we identify what could get in the way of achieving the results we want the greater the likelihood we will succeed. From fairy tales to real life, the endings are never quite what we anticipate.

## Correcting and Monitoring Your Action Plan

Included in your action plan are ways to evaluate your progress. How will you know you are on track unless you have specific milestones upon which you can measure your results? A milestone specifies what you will do by when. If you struggle with how to balance your career with your home life, when you design your action plan you may decide that in the first month, you'll spend thirty days observing how much and what kinds of projects you delegate to your staff. You may want to observe the opinions you make about your employees or yourself in terms of their competence and ability versus yours. Or you may ask yourself if controlling what happens in your department is a direct result of the interference you feel from your superiors.

Once you have accumulated raw data, you can ask yourself what gets in the way to delegating more work to staff, to spending more time coaching young recruits to take on more responsibility, or to sharing your ideas of how others can support your leadership. There are many ways to untangle the knots we have created. Noticing is the first step. Conducting observations, participating in coaching programs provide participants with a valuable commodity—reflection. Because we move so quickly in our lives, the art of reflection is lost.

It's a lot easier to delegate work when you feel confident with peoples' competence to perform. If you have given yourself six months to re-frame your work life so you can have more balance with your family, you can set specific goals each month for what time you will leave the office. Again, old habits die hard. If you find yourself moving the clock back because of some important crisis or call then you might want to find someone in your organization who is really adept at setting and holding boundaries. The person who leaves at the same time each day can serve as your support system so you can build the muscle to leave on time, too. The key to success is flexibility, but flexibility within the context of your vision.

> *Keep an eye on your vision but be willing to dance with Life.*
>
> **Zen Saying**

There are several things to monitor as you engage in your project:

- Your own resistance to change.
- Your results as you do the practices.

Bringing your actions into alignment with your vision takes time. Some people make dramatic first steps in the overhaul process. Others work methodically, peeling away the layers of habits and judgments blocking their true selves. It takes a while for the person you wish to become to emerge from the many years of the person you have created.

If you find resistance to change is getting in the way, what action(s) can you take? Many people give up the change effort because they initially fail in their efforts to either do the practices they instituted or they don't see changes happening fast enough. Welcome to the club! We all experience fits and starts when we step into unfamiliar territory. Be kind to yourself.

Why not experiment with your resistance to change? Try visiting your own resistance as if it is a foreign country with which you are unfamiliar. Study the landscape of your resistance, including the language (what you tell yourself and others), the emotions (expressed to the world or rolling around your head) as well as the physical sensations in your body as you resist. Greet your resistance with curiosity. The beauty of being able to reinvent ourselves at any age is we get to experiment. But only if we give ourselves permission to play, to see, to not see anything at all, to succeed or to fail. Pay attention! As you play the tourist role with your resistance, ask yourself, "What is this resistance about? How is it constructed? How does it work in my life?"

By investigating your resistance you will better know if the resistance is a defense mechanism or truly an important message worth heeding. Look for clues. Does your resistance feel like you're digging your heels into the ground, stubbornly refusing to move from your spot? Or has something just happened, like a broken arm that is temporarily throwing you off kilter? Remember my workaholic client who presently cannot see his way to include balance (self –care) in his life? As much as we say we want our lives to be different many of us will hold onto to what we have, even if it's killing us. If you're arguing that loudly for your position, you are probably resisting.

Monitor your results regularly. Check in with yourself, whether you do it quietly in a meditative state or by journaling what you are noticing. Trust that you will know when the results are right because they will feel and look right to you.

## Completing and Reviewing The Project

A project is complete when the conditions for fulfillment have been met. Who determines the conditions for fulfillment? You do. Or you can put someone else in charge who will define and recognize the actual outcomes as initially identified in the project outline. Whoever determines the end of the program can also evaluate the program's effectiveness.

Reviewing your participation, milestones, and outcomes will give you a good picture of what worked and didn't work. Completing a project enables us to review lessons learned, insights gained, breakdowns resolved. Not only does conducting a review help us close the door on what we've have done, it also gives us a chance to identify what's been omitted from the project that still needs follow up or completion, now, or in the future.

Several years ago I was participating with employees in a long term consulting project. They were very skillful identifying the need to design and implement a program; they did monitor their performance throughout, but when it came time to review their work, they were already tackling the next project. They did not want to take any more time to review their actions or lessons learned. I was wondering if this was a condition that prevailed only with this group, so I did a little detective work in the other organizations where I coached.

By informally surveying other groups, I discovered that once a goal has been attained, or the project shelved, managers are already focused on what's next. The idea of taking time to reflect on lessons learned, or even acknowledge the contributions of players seemed like a time waster.

I began to notice that organizations incurred recurring breakdowns in operations simply because they had not taken the time to conduct a review of their work, from how the work had impacted the organization or met the customers' needs. People were off and running to what's next and pressing. Always in a crisis mode, employees had no downtime to review. They might criticize some steps taken during the process but once completed, they simply moved on. What amazed me was the constant shifting of priorities or problems that needed immediate attention. How people worked was important while people were involved in the project, but unless there was some security, safety or legal breach, most folks finished, and moved on.

Some groups forget to monitor and correct their performance because the focus in on getting the job done on time. The results might not be spectacular, the customer might not be satisfied, but the job has been done. Since these employees did not take time to review either their performance or their outcomes, they forgot or lost sight of the many breakdowns they incurred along the way. They ended up carrying recurring problems from one project to another. And they looked at their problems as part of the overall institutional madness they had to live with in order to have a secure job.

We lose sight of what we hold dear when we move from one project to the next without taking the time to acknowledge the fulfillment of our vision. We lose sight of our contributions or our connection to something bigger than the project we have just finished because we don't take the time to acknowledge how what we have done relates to the big picture. Over time, we become disconnected from our vision.

Although these steps may seem methodical, or too tedious to do, over time the review process becomes second nature.

## Practice Gratitude or Appreciation

When we begin a reinvention process we are intent on getting it done, seeing it through--even hoping for the best. We never know when we start the journey exactly where we will end up. We don't even know if we will have a happy or happier ending. How do we keep ourselves on track when we can't see light at the end of the tunnel? My friend Stephanie Abramson suggests that I look at each problem or each obstacle as a lesson from which I can learn. She supports me to greet the problem with appreciation.

Her approach allows me to disengage emotionally from what I am complaining about to be able to reflect on what is actually happening. I am grateful for her support. I am grateful to be able to let go the anxiety I let fester regarding my successes and failures.

I believe that to become the kind of person you say is worth becoming, practicing gratitude is essential. We do not actualize our dreams by ourselves. We do not live in this world by ourselves. We may feel isolated, separated or even disconnected, by language, culture, race, religion, education, or political views, but really we are more connected to each other than we even realize. I keep seeing and feeling this connection as I step into organizations where at first I'm an outsider, and over time, a partner. Reinvention is the work of a lifetime. I keep adapting the words from my improvisation teacher, Rick Fiori:

*"**Be one hundred percent committed to the part you play.
Be honest.
Tell a story."***

Practice gratitude for yourself and for any person or thing without whose touch on your life, you would be a far sorrier human being.

**When all else fails, " Fake it till you make it."**

# Section Three: Competence

CHAPTER NINE:

# It's Like Riding A Bicycle

*We are what we repeatedly do. Excellence, therefore, is not an act, but a habit.*

*Aristotle*

## Why Are Competencies Important?

### The Honorable Judge Moody Tidwell, (Retired), U.S. Court of Federal Claims

*"I think part of what happens to us, especially when we reach a certain level in our profession is that we start to take ourselves seriously, like we really do know what we are doing because that's why we are here making this kind of money."*

Competencies, or the combination of skills and knowledge, form the last side of the reinvention triangle. Why donate a chapter to competence? We need all three elements to bring our vision to life. When I first started coaching, I worked with Ellen, a very talented graphics designer who wanted to make money. She brought some unique skills to her graphics business, but the downside was not her lack of artistry or her inability to structure a home- based business rather it was the fear of talking to people about what she could offer.

It was a vicious cycle because she could effectively translate her client's vision into beautiful graphics, but she was unwilling to get on the phone to market her services, or even network with people who could hire her. She didn't feel comfortable asking for referrals. When a project ended with a client, she was left scrambling for money until a new one fell into her lap. We worked on strengthening her competence to market and communicate her skills to produce steady, consistent income.

Many of us would rather focus our attention on that which we do well, or that which we know, rather than try to learn something new. We don't like failing, we don't like looking silly and we especially don't like being in situations where we feel a loss of control. Ellen was a talented graphics designer, but who cares if no one knows she's available? The value of working with a coach is that you're being supported, guided by someone who knows how to get you to the results you want.

Clients are not alone as they face their demons or their angels. Coaches will create a step- by- step process you can begin that will, over time, get you the results. That is the big difference between learning how to do something from a book and learning how to do something under the watchful eye of a coach. Coaches will observe how you play on the field and prescribe a practice that is right for you at the right time.

Learning how to market one's results takes practice. Ellen argued for her limitations, rather than put herself in a learning mode. She felt more comfortable suffering as an under-appreciated graphics designer than engaging in a practice that would save her business. I think we all fall into this hole from time to time. For a variety of reasons we cannot bring ourselves to take on the learning that is necessary. If you want the results bad enough you will find the inner strength to take effective action.

A popular rationale for not developing our competence to perform is lack of time. "I don't have the time to develop myself so that I can play my best." Again, we make Time the enemy. Why are we so willing to accept less of ourselves? We are snagged by a sense of futility about having what we really want. Or we capitulate to a pressing fear that having what we want in life doesn't really matter. When we give up on our dreams, we give up on ourselves.

I've had a coaching business for two decades. Similar to any skilled professional I have spent years learning my craft in various classroom settings, years apprenticing to more experienced coaches and have successfully served as a journeyman in my field. Mastery of any craft takes patience, passion, a skillful teacher and a willingness to accept where we are, no matter where we are.

When I was learning how to coach, I tended to overlook building a business. Since being financially independent is integral to my vision of what is worth doing, I realized I had to strengthen my competence to build a referral- based business. I did not necessarily like what I uncovered in my self- assessment, but at least I have a foundation upon which I can build. Currently, I know where I stand as related to where I wish to be.

We all have blind spots in our thinking. That's what makes us human. Of course since I arrogantly believe I know what's best for myself I did tell myself, even scold myself that I could figure out the riddle of how to continuously build a coaching business-- myself. Why do we spend time going in circles trying to solve puzzles we don't have the skills to solve? Some of us have convinced ourselves that we "should" or "ought" to know what it takes or know what to do *because*...

After knocking my head against the wall for several years trying to figure out what was "wrong" with my marketing skills, and how come with all my credentials I couldn't earn a decent living, I decided to hire some experts to help. By asking for help, I removed the pressure I had placed on myself. One of the best business lessons I've learned is that I can either take the time and energy to develop the competence required or I can save myself the anxiety of learning and hire a pro.

Each time you get into the *"because story"* of why life is the way it is, or why things happen the way they do, you are headed down a phony path in the woods. Telling myself repeatedly that I "should" know what it takes to build a business did not free me to take effective action. In fact, I end up feeling guilty, ashamed or frustrated. Worse, I still couldn't move my business in the direction I was seeking.

Even coaches get the blues.

## Coaching Exercise:

**Instructions:** You have the vision of what is worth doing. You have outlined systems or structures that will support you to bring your vision to life. Now you can identify the skills you will need to tie the package together.

1. Identify one area of your life that you believe is worth improving or enhancing as it relates to your overall dream of how you want your life to look.
2. What it's going to take in terms of time, money and resources to accomplish your goal?
3. What skills will you need for your project to succeed?
4. What's your current knowledge base as it applies to this project?
5. What's missing in your knowledge base that if you had the information would move you forward to achieve?
6. Who or what sources are available from whom you can learn or apprentice?
7. What outcomes are you seeking from spending time or money to learn what you need?

CHAPTER TEN:

# Sound Off

*"All you need to do is point and shoot"*

**Old Kodak camera advertisement**

## Dr. Richard Barnett, National Basketball Association, New York Knicks, Retired

*"You are always evolving. You just don't change. Life is about change. Everybody is going to change, whether it's for the better or for the worst. A lot of people don't want to face the truth. The truth can be harsh. I am an advocate of George Bernard Shaw who said, "I dream things that never were and ask why not?" You have to be willing to pay the price to pursue your dreams. You can't get there going home, kicking back and drinking a beer."*

### *What is Competence?*

Competencies are the skills and knowledge needed to perform a task. Using my weight loss experience as our learning model, I educated myself about food, including the contents of various foods and their impact on my system. Some people argue that losing weight is simply possessing the resolve to not eat fattening foods, but I found that resolve was only my first step. Educating myself about the values inherent in different kinds of foods sustained my weight loss efforts. Initially, much of my weight loss was a product of saying "no," breaking familiar eating patterns, at home and in public.

However as I implemented new eating habits, saying "no" became easier and less of an intervention. Eating healthier, planning and shopping for the "right" foods, monitoring my eating habits and my moods, seeing my clothes fit better all contributed to helping me bring my vision of how I wanted to look-- to life.

What skills did I need to acquire to lose the weight? Everything from food shopping to food preparation, to problem solving as I integrated the information I gleaned in weekly Weight Watcher sessions into my daily life. Plus, I honed my communication skills, from reading to listening. I had to learn how to hear the feedback I was receiving from weight loss counselors, other participants, my family and myself. Specific constructive feedback guided me to keep correcting my behaviors around food. With all the information flooding the market on weight loss, I really didn't know much

Weight Watchers provided a structure and some guidance. Much of my learning came from listening to other participants. Most of the time I was on automatic pilot regarding my body. I'm vain, so I looked at myself all the time, but I felt quite helpless to make the kinds of changes I needed. I had to learn how to manually operate myself so that I could successfully create the end result.

Seeing the relationship between my moods and my eating patterns gave me courage to keep persevering with my program. I can say, after many years, with several diet breakdowns, I've increased my effectiveness to monitor and correct my weight so that I am more in alignment with my vision of good health. I play the weight loss game more from how I want to be in my life, than playing from my reaction to things not going my way, or being unhappy, etc. In fact, like the veteran athletes interviewed for this book, I play more from the neck up than the shoulders down. But do I always win? No.

By paying careful attention to events, people and my own core beliefs about myself, I can gauge when, where and how my old eating patterns will kick into gear. It doesn't take much to fall off the wagon or end up standing in front of the open fridge. First I learned interventions. In time I learned new habits. Finally, I became a different person in relationship to food.

To get the most from my attendance and participation in weight loss programs, I slowly let down my defenses protecting my image of who I thought I was. By accepting guidance, advice and even support from fellow weight loss players, I began enjoying the game I was playing. I did not have to know or pretend to know everything about how to be healthy and slim in life. I only had to be willing to learn what I needed to play my best. My willingness to keep learning despite my tendency to judge my efforts good or bad, or my emotional mood swings between " I'm doing great" or "I'm never going to get there!" enabled me to stay the course of my dreams.

What comes first the chicken or the egg?" I never did understand what my mother meant, but I believed that she had access to some deep truth about life. What comes first, the vision or the skills? Although I think having a vision of what is worth doing or becoming supports us to focus on the skills we need to bring our vision to life, I have observed from my interviews that there are times when strengthening our skills results in our increased desire to become a" something" or a" someone". Vision is the picture of what we want, structure is how we get there and competencies are what it takes.

For my friend Moody Tidwell, traveling to South Africa to serve as a mediator between warring tribes permitted him to live more of his vision for the American courts. He is translating his experience with warring factions into his courtroom; his listening skills have deepened. His commitment to bringing peace to South Africa is mirrored in his passion for bringing excellence in communication to his courtroom.

Maybe you begin journal writing as a way to reduce stress and end up five years later writing plays as an avocation. Who really knows for sure if the skills you are learning in mid-life can help you forge the next life you undertake? We're in a continuous process of reshaping our thinking, our lives, and our relationships to others. Sometimes we are intentionally designing a new path, other times we are designing unintentionally. *Navigating Tomorrow* is a formula for intentionally developing the skills and knowledge you will need to create a new life.

## The Honorable Moody Tidwell, Judge, (Retired), U. S. Federal Claims Court

*"To be excellent in my field requires intelligence, patience and integrity. Living up to my oath to apply the laws of the land fairly. It's integrity and commitment in your word. You bring integrity listening to people, both witnesses and attorneys. Without integrity the legal system fails, which means the whole government, the whole structure, the whole country would fail. Judges have to apply the law whether or not they believe it's right in a certain case or not. There is a constant dialogue gong on the in the courtroom. Discover the facts of the case and look at each one fresh. Listen without a pre-conceived bias or with the knowledge that you do have*

*a pre-conceived bias and put that aside. My vision is to make the American Judicial System better-- either better than it is now or implement a structure by which I won't do it any harm.*

*I really think that business, including my business, is all about relationships. If you turn around and empower your employees, giving them the authority to run the business, you're building a relationship with them. You have to hire the people you trust and then get out of their way. It's not like I'm going to support my staff to make mistakes, rather, I know that mistakes will happen, but if I do all the leg work up front and use the resources that are available and be willing to learn form my mistakes, that is a very human way to run a business.*

*I don't think you can tell people to show respect, but you can teach people about respect by giving them the space to be themselves, giving them the freedom to speak, the freedom to speak responsibly by letting them know you are not there to listen to trivia. We are here to do a job, and I'm going to permit the people in my courtroom to do their job to the best of their abilities. You can't teach people these qualities; you have to show them how to do that. To get people to produce for you, you have to treat them with respect, accepting a person for who they are and what they are. I give them an opening to be themselves, rather than having to be a certain way for me. It's easier to be this way than to project through body language or tone a sense of derision or cynicism that shuts people up. If I'm doing my job I sit up there and listen. I control the triumph. They control their case."*

### What is The Difference between Skills and Qualities?

**Skills: The things we learn so we can "do" something.**
**Qualities: The traits we develop so we can "become" someone.**

What do skills and qualities have in common? They both require practice. Once you learn a skill or develop a quality, you cannot sit back on your laurels. Without regular ongoing practice our newly acquired skills become rusty; our qualities become tainted.

To distinguish between skills and qualities is to view skills as that which you do and qualities as how you practice your thoughts, speech and action In business we talk a lot about qualities that are important to our success with employees and customers. Qualities we identify include: respect, caring, generosity, acceptance, patience trust, and honesty. We salute local, national and international heroes who espouse these qualities.

We spend endless training dollars identifying the qualities we wish to exhibit organizationally, and then we spend no training dollars developing these qualities in our employees. Many feel that these qualities "ought" or "should" be cultivated in the home, not in the workplace. Others feel that you can't teach qualities to people. This group claims that people either possess the quality or they don't. Many of us don't want to step into discussions about our level of honesty, trust or respect with employees because we feel that what we will uncover might make all of us uncomfortable. We hope that by identifying the qualities we seek in people they will find their own way to embody them. Often we identify qualities without modeling them ourselves.

If we approach the development or enhancement of qualities the same way we approach the development of skills we might be more effective creating the desired results. When you picture yourself being more patient, in specific situations or with certain kinds of people, and you have a sense of what being patient looks like or feels like, and how others might respond to you if you were more patient, then you can put practices into place that will nurture the development of this quality. Developing patience may take a lot longer than developing computer skills, but the rewards of increased patience for self and others will spill over to all areas of your life.

What if we removed the label of "soft" from the study and development of qualities, and instead viewed the development of skills and qualities as two sides of the same coin? To develop qualities, we look at our thoughts, speech and action. The same way we conducted self-observation exercises to review our systems, we can also observe how often or not we are patient, or kind, or honest. Many folks resign themselves to accepting they can't have or develop these qualities. We assume we either have them or we don't. But that belief has more to do with not knowing where to look, or what to look for.

I am a product of the work I have been doing on myself. I believe I can change how I live in life, and how I wish to be. This whole book is based on the premise that any person can reinvent himself from the inside out if he or she has the desire, forges a commitment and does the work.

For the most part we don't teach, train or develop qualities. Most of us (adults) do not have the faintest idea how to cultivate specific qualities like patience or trust. We mean well, we try hard, but we don't have daily or weekly practices to strengthen these qualities in ourselves. Most of us don't have the time to investigate how patient or impatient we are in life. We simply accept our bad habits as part of our makeup. We hope that others will accept both our strengths and weaknesses. We are grateful when we meet a patient and kind person. We are especially grateful when this same person extends this patience to us. The whole point about *Navigating Tomorrow* is that who we are now is not who we need to be in the future. Moment to moment we get to choose how we wish to be or how we wish to interact with life.

Engaging in practices that strengthen skills and qualities support our efforts to continually develop into the kind of person we wish to be. Waving the wand does not work! Writing and publishing organizational visions alone will not yield the "being" qualities we seek. Hoping for change does not produce results.

Just because other people in the organization do not practice kindness, patience or respect does not mean I have to be the same way. In the end I live with myself. No matter how many nooks and crannies, no matter how good the con, at any moment in the day, we are alone with ourselves. It may take all the patience I have to be patient with people who are distrustful, anxious, or unkind. I keep reminding myself that I am on the path to becoming the kind of person I most want to be. When we take on new practices, we are committing and often re-committing to investing our resources in ourselves.

There is an integral relationship between our thoughts, speech and action. The more I do something, the more adept I become. The more adept I become at something, the better I feel. The better I feel the more expansive or available I am for myself and for others. Developing our technical skills does not necessarily translate to becoming open, caring and trusting. This is a double- edged conversation.

In organizations, managers reward technical excellence by promoting the person to a supervisory position. The technical expert may possess/exhibit few or no relationship skills. The new organization he leads begins a downward spiral. Why? Because his employees don't feel the "love" or appreciation required to keep giving their best. Senior leaders begin hammering on the technical expert to do better. He, like my graphics person wants to be successful but has no clue how to extend himself or foster relationships with others. On his own he can create miracles but has no inkling how to collaborate.

## Barbara Roberts, Former Governor of Oregon

*"I came from a household where respect for others was really important. We were taught to tell the truth. The expectation in a respecting household is that people tell the truth. That's how you treat people. My father thought I had value even though I was girl, and at that time, Dads wanted sons. But I grew up feeling very special. In the political arena, I wanted that same thing. You don't get respect unless you give respect, and you cannot give respect to people if you lie to them, if you cheat them, if you are dishonest with them or manipulate them.*

*If you don't trust them enough to tell them the truth, either the voters or your colleagues, you lose them. I think when you come into the political system with a cause your approach is a little bit different because you don't see your steps as career building. You can't change everybody in the world. Only person you can control is you. If I can influence others by being a good role model, by being the kind of path breaker, setting an example is a wonderful way to change any system. If you are courageous enough to set that kind of example, it's a lot easier for others to join you".*

## Mike Dukakis, Former Governor of Massachusetts & Presidential Candidate

*"Most politicians are pretty competitive. We know we are in a race, and we run hard. We want to win because we believe deeply in what we believe. We want to have the opportunity to do something about what we believe. Is winning better than losing? You bet. Do you learn something from losing? Yes.*

*I became a better listener. I began understanding that you cannot get things done in public life without building coalitions, without involving people actively and genuinely in what you are doing and having respect for them. The best solution to the dilemma of weighing what people say before you act is to have a clear sense of what you want to do at the onset. If you want to do very important things, do them. But at the same time, be a coalition and consensus builder. The best people in the business can do both".*

CHAPTER ELEVEN:

# Practice, Practice, Practice

*The game ain't over till it's over—*

*Yogi Berra*

***Practice, Practice, Practice***

*I'd rather learn from one bird
how to sing, then to teach ten thousand stars
how not to dance.*
**e.e. cummings**

When I was in my early forties I was forced to vacate my rental apartment; fortunately, my friend Melissa needed the extra rental income. Sharing housekeeping duties and our lives made sense. As colleagues in the coaching profession, we felt strongly that we could forge a living arrangement that supported both of us.

Even though I was doing yoga and aerobics, I kept a couple of vices, one of which included smoking cigarettes. Although I didn't smoke a lot, I enjoyed unwinding at the end of workday with a cigarette. Most days I smoked outside. One weekend, Melissa went out of town, leaving me in charge of the house and her cats. We had a cardinal rule not to smoke in the house, but with no one at home, I felt mischievous. Who would know except me? I lit up, dropped the match into the waste- basket under my desk and went upstairs to make a cup of coffee.

As I was sitting on the sofa in the living room waiting for the coffee to brew, I noticed smoke coming out of the fireplace. At first I thought nothing of it but something made me stand up to investigate. I couldn't smell anything. Nothing was burning on the stove. Now smoke was billowing from the fireplace. I walked to the top of the stairs that led to the basement and to my horror saw my desk engulfed in flames. I can't explain in words what happened in the moment I registered disaster. It's as if I became light and heavy at the same time. I felt rooted by the sight of flames spreading; I could feel the panic beginning to cause tremors in my legs and stomach. For what seemed like a long time, I didn't move. I was already leaving my body behind. I have seen flames before, but never in a house.

All kinds of thoughts poured into my consciousness. My senses felt alive. I was completely alert, yet totally unaware. I thought if I could just get by the flames to my bedroom I could save my new fur coat and my diamond ring. Or I could run over to the couch in front of the fiery desk to salvage my purse. But then another force moved me back upstairs to find the cats and leave.

I ran out to the street yelling for help. I was calling out to the neighbors that my house was on fire. My neighbors called 911. In just a matter of minutes, firemen were at the scene, breaking windows throwing plants and chairs through the bay window to the yard. I know I stood out in the driveway the whole time firemen worked to save the house; somehow my brain stepped in to protect me from my feelings. It was January 21 1991, a brutally cold day to be standing in jeans and a tee shirt.

The fire chief's investigation determined that the match from my cigarette had ignited the papers in the waste- basket. Something small, and harmless turned my life upside down. I was still in a trance. Since my roommate was out of town, I had another twenty-four hours to figure out how I would tell her that the home she had opened to me had burned. Yes, my life was upside down, but she had a child, a dog, two cats, and no place to live. The firemen boarded the house.

A friend/coaching client volunteered to house me. What a strange feeling to walk away from your life. I left the cats, asking neighbors to keep an eye out for them.  Sitting in my friend's basement, next to her washer and dryer, I called my family in Canada and calmly explained how I just lost everything I owned. The trance was all encompassing. I think when disaster strikes, at least for some of us the pain is so complete we don't actually feel anything, like pain or sorrow. We are simply standing off kilter as the world we have known spins away.

We move through simple daily activities, but we're not connected to anything. All I had known or cherished was gone. I floated through the aftermath of the fire with some sense of logic, filling out insurance forms, rummaging through charred clothing, holding my breath, sighing deeply.

I dreaded returning to the house. Borrowing a jacket from my friend, I drove back to the house the next day. The night air was cold, distant. I sat in my car waiting for my roommate to return. When she pulled into the driveway, with her daughter and dog in tow, I greeted her with the "good news bad news routine." The front door was boarded. We pulled off the boards, entering the house by flashlight. God bless her, she didn't cry. The air was thick, rancid with smoke. I tried to make myself invisible because I felt responsible for upsetting her life. She went to another neighbor's house to make phone calls to find a place for her and her daughter to stay. She didn't yell or scream. In fact, she handled the whole situation quite diplomatically. We were both nomads at this point. I left her and returned to basement haven.

When we met again during that next week, it was in the house, rummaging around the rubbish of our lives. Since the fire had started in my living area, all my belongings were too charred to save. My friend's belongings had suffered extensive smoke damage. My fur coat, though still intact, had been exposed to the extreme heat of the fire. I was not ready to give up my coat, so I placed it in a large green garbage bag and drove it around in the trunk of my car for several weeks until I could part with it.

My rings were safe, as were my car keys. The melted black rubber of my ignition key is a gentle reminder of the heat of that Sunday.

I thought I was losing my best friend. We would pass each other in the halls of the house, she walking in with her sisters or friends, me wandering aimlessly in search of some memento. Since the electricity and water had been turned off we saw each other in dark shadows, through the haze of frigid cold, dampness from water drenched clothing and furniture, and the acrid smell of smoke that lingered throughout. We would barely speak as we worked our way from room to room trying to find something we could salvage.

My guilt increased each time we met. What could I do about the damage to our home? There was no joy I could give her. I blamed myself for being the "bad" girl; she blamed me for upsetting her tranquil life. I tried to practice forgiveness for my sins, but I could see no way to free myself.

Although the fire was ruled accidental, I knew that my behavior had led to disaster. And yet, in the middle of such grave sorrow, she blessed me by saying, "Everything I really needed I carried in my head and in my heart." This line, tossed so lightly in the middle of such pain helped me find my balance as the structure of my life disintegrated. My friend was practicing kindness in spite of her understandable anger.

Although our interactions were perfunctory, we both kept up our practices as best we could. January 21 1991 is still a blur, but I do know that our efforts to be the kind of people we respected, our willingness to walk through this tragedy together, knowing we would survive helped us right ourselves as Spring replaced Winter. About two months after the fire, we met for lunch. I could feel the tension between us. I wanted Melissa to forgive me, but there was so much anger and resentment that neither of us were in a place to truly be kind. The most merciful act we did was to give each other the space to heal our wounds. As she spoke I could feel myself stretching internally to hold onto her words. There was no bitterness; we were both feeling out the experience.

The mind chatter began while Melissa spoke, but I kept breathing and exhaling, breathing and exhaling, and began to sense relief in myself. I knew I would be okay, that she loved me, and that at this moment she had to walk away from our friendship. I appreciated her wisdom. For this kindness, I was most grateful. I would have kept turning myself into knots to be loved by her. I decided to let go of every expectation I had about what we could do to save our friendship. It took all the trust and faith I felt.

What happened? We healed. We went our own separate paths for almost a year. I found another place to live, quite enjoying the newness of life without clothes, furniture or books. My whole life fit into my compact car. Was this an easy road back for each of us? I maintain that doing yoga, meditation, and aerobics on a regular basis provided some stability for each us when neither of us had any stability. I also believe that giving other people the time they need to heal is one of the greatest gifts we can bestow

But in order to let go, we have to let go.

In the years since the fire we've asked each other what allowed us to come back together in a deeper and more powerful way. All we can say is that we listened to the sorrow we each carried, we respected how we each dealt with the blow, and we gave one another space to grow, to heal to grow again. We left the devastation of our life, we planted seeds where we could, we nourished each other the best we could, and we moved on.

I did quit smoking.

### *Practice, Practice, Practice…*

*"You can change everything except death."*
                                                      **Arlene the Therapist**

What supports our ability to begin and sustain a practice depends on three conditions: our reliance upon a network of support, the structure around which we can add or include a practice and finally, a level of commitment or willingness to engage in the practice despite how we feel about what we are doing as we are doing it. We do become that which we practice. I have become so accustomed to regular exercise that included in how I relate in life is body movement. It's as if my body knows when it's time to work out. Clients will tell me about the times they did specific
practices to reduce stress or increase creativity only to stop doing these practice(s) once they had achieved certain benefits.

Why do we stop doing the things that create such positive benefits for us? The catch about practices is they work because we do them. Practices also provide feedback.

One of my clients wants to move into a leadership position, but he spends his time doing the technical part of his job with which he is familiar, instead of taking on higher risk projects that are outside his comfort zone. He cannot leap from one way of working in life to another. We must design some practice steps he can take that will over time build his competence to lead. In addition, we'll have to insure that he has a network of support upon whose guidance he can rely. We have brainstormed together to identify a handful of potential advocates both inside his organization and in other public agencies. Just telling him what he already knows, that taking on additional leadership responsibilities is a smart thing to do doesn't help because in his current state, he doesn't have the wherewithal to take on the duties. He would if he could. Therefore, as his coach, I'm designing several kinds of exercises that will help him both shape the leadership stance he wishes to establish, as well as provide strengthening practices for those leadership qualities that are weak.

What are some of the activities he is doing? He spends time reading about people whose leadership style he respects. He has identified and is better able to communicate his strengths to others. To loosen him up, he has enrolled in improvisation classes where in a safe and fun environment he can tap into his creative/fun side. Improvisation is loosening his concern about "expressing himself".

By playing different roles and seeing that nothing bad happens when he takes risks, he will more easily step into the role he wishes to play. He is networking both with managers in his organization and throughout other agencies where he has the potential to lead. He is also outlining a blueprint of the kind of work he would love to do and sharing this blueprint with his manager. We have worked together for more than a year. It has taken several months for him to integrate his practices in his daily life. I am learning patience as we work together. Not all people move at the same rate; my sense of urgency might not equate to his.

Many of us want our lives to be different but the actions we undertake are so incongruent to how we live that we fail, which only makes us feel worse about our condition. Reinvention is not about tips and techniques.

## Rickie C. Harris, National Football League, Retired
## Played for the Washington Redskins 1965-1969

*"If you want success in any part of your life, social or professional you have to come to practice every day so you can play. The more you play the better you get. When I played football, the more unselfish I became, the better my team played. Then because the team got better, I had more of a desire to be unselfish. We ended up reaching the goal-- which was a winning season. I never realized that showing up every day in my social life was like coming to football- practice. I have learned as I have rebuilt my life after drugs that I have all the ingredients I need to handle whatever challenge life brings me. It can't be anything I haven't already face".*

### *Practice, Practice, Practice*

## Gary Green- Youngest National Hockey League Coach, Hockey Analyst

*"What you need as a business owner, you also need as a coach. You need communication skills, resources, ethics and morals. You have to focus on achieving, as well as how you develop pride in your product, pride in your team. You better not assume that all your players are performing at their maximum. Teach your players to be better, give them the opportunity to improve, make sure they are prepared.*

*Hockey players practice 4 or 5 days a week before their big game. But in business, you don't give yourselves the chance to practice before that presentation before a new client. You scramble, put it together, go out and present and analyze afterwards. That's where hockey players differ from business players. As a coach I wouldn't expect people to win on the field, unless I gave them prep time. I understand the margin in business. I know that if I am going to have the system work for employees, we all have to sacrifice something. Will we make those sacrifices to have our lives work? I don't know."*

The easiest way to develop competence in any one area is by identifying the skills and knowledge it takes to perform that activity. Painting the picture of the activity being done well helps you design practices that improve performance.

Let's revisit my client who has a dream of moving up the corporate ladder in the organization but ends up spending his time resolving recurring administrative nightmares because that's what he thinks he does best. Plus, he is good problem solver. As his dream has shifted to being recognized by the organization as a leader, not simply as a technical support person, he knows that he has to view himself differently, change some of what he spends time doing, and demonstrate to others that he is a leader.

As I said earlier in the chapter, encouraging him to network informally with leaders in his organization will give him information about the actions others have taken. He will analyze his findings and design a blueprint for action. If he studies his organization, both looking at the strategic plans, vision and current operation goals, he will also widen his lens to see more than just the details of his job. As he builds bridges with senior managers, he will begin to see the bigger picture of his organization, as well as his role in defining, refining and bringing the picture to life.

How does he become more of a risk taker? Doing weekly improvisation will strengthen his 'courage' muscle as he engages himself fully with others. Leaders have to be willing to take risks. If he knows he needs to get into the ring but he has avoided putting himself in to a position where he might be uncomfortable, then strengthening his trust muscle will support him to move in the direction he wants. Not all practices have to be done in the workplace to be effective. What other activities would you encourage my technician to do?

When I teach *The Art of Winning* classes, participants let me know that winning means:

1. Playing their best
2. Achieving their goals

3. Feeling happy in themselves
4. Doing what they love

Very few people talk about winning or losing, rather they wish they had more control or balance in their daily lives. They want to have systems in place that will support their efforts to work, balance home and career, and take care of themselves. When I first began writing this book I knew that I had within myself the capability to play my best. I already had a picture of how I wanted to live. I had lost my best friend, experienced the sense of failure and loss, released my expectations and judgments about myself, and then spent some time regaining my balance.

I am not going to say that life is always one way or the other, good or bad, because that isn't true. Not only do we want to control our own destiny, many of us would like to control the others' destinies as well. We believe if we can figure out how the game works, whatever the game is, we will win. But life doesn't work that way. I wish it did. What I've discovered by using this process is that because I have a clear picture of how I wish to live and because I have developed and implemented practices that support me to bring my vision to life, when I hit a storm, I can right myself fairly quickly. It is no longer about controlling the events or people in my life, because at any moment the control can be wrestled from me.

The best bet is to learn how to live fully in the present. You can wait until you are thrown into the pit to fight your way out, or else you can keep nurturing yourself so that no matter how you are tossed in life, you will find your footing quickly. Engaging in a variety of practices, from meditation to dance, all contribute to building a stable base upon which you can stand.

Sometimes the steps we take to reinvent our lives are quantum leaps, other times, we move at a slow, yet steady pace. *Navigating Tomorrow* is not about tips and techniques. The people interviewed for this book created winning lives based upon persistence, faith and a commitment to something bigger than themselves. Nor were their lives fairy tales. They have all hit highs and lows, and have chosen to keep going.

And then they started over. There is no magic bullet to reinventing the self. There is study and experimentation. The people interviewed gave themselves permission to create and to play.

My friend Dan, a shop teacher in a Virginia high school recently pointed out that his mission was to provide students the chance to fail. He loves when his students make the effort, when they move beyond their fears of failure to try. He has a created a learning environment where students can play as they learn. " They come into my class, wanting to do it right every time. Life doesn't work that way," he points out, "How will you know if what you are doing is going to work if you don't give yourself the chance to fail, as well as succeed?"

## Coaching Exercise: Designing Baby Steps

**Instructions:** Pick one area of your life where you wish you had greater skill to perform a task related to your vision Or pick a quality you wish to enhance, like courage, patience, or honesty.

After you select an area take the following baby steps:

1. Find at least two people who embody or express a quality or skill you wish you had.
2. Set up lunch or dinner with them. During the meal ask them how they got to be the way they are. Ask as many questions as you need so you will have a good picture of how they define a particular quality or skill, where they use it, how they keep that skill alive or vital in themselves, etc.
3. Ask them if they will mentor you so you can develop this skill or quality (optional).
4. If you move ahead with a mentoring relationship, outline, up front what you both can expect from the relationship. For example: Talk about time lines, ways of communicating (phone, in person, email), Be willing to flex your muscles, Structure the relationship so that it works for both parties. Be creative with mentors, not cheap.
5. If you opt out of the mentoring relationship, ask them what suggestions or steps they would recommend for you. Listen.
6. Look for alternative ways you can work together without the commitment of mentoring. Will they serve as advisors as part of an informal advisory team you design? Can you call them with specific concerns related to this topic? Explore what you can do together.
7. Ask them to help you clarify your desired outcomes. What would they see for instance, if you were more skillful in a particular area? The more specific you can be when designing outcomes, the easier it is to monitor and correct yourself along the way.

I often recommend clients conduct a self- observation in a particular area they wish to strengthen. The more we know how we react or act in specific situations, the easer it becomes to design a "corrective" strategy to change our behaviors. Self- observations are useful because they provide current, up- to- date information about our habits and patterns. You can't change what you don't know.

For example, if a person knows she has to take better care of herself, but has no idea how to begin, I might suggest that she observes how often in her day she makes requests for help. At the end of two weeks this person will have a lot of examples of how she either takes on more responsibilities or shies away from asking for help. Together we review the data collected. Then we co-create a strategy that will support her to make effective requests, delegate more tasks to others while at the same time, leaving earlier to go to the yoga class to which she's already enrolled.

## Gary Green- Youngest National Hockey League Coach, Hockey Analyst

*"As a broadcaster, I have been able to do my broadcasting and run other businesses at same time. And I have had a wide variety of businesses. Some successful, some not successful. I have learned that the first time when I meet people through networking etc. who tell me that they have golden touch, that they have had unbelievable success in business, that they have been fortunate with no failures, I don't spend any time with that person, because they are probably lying. Understanding and doing those things that make you a good coach, also make you a good business owner. You can be a good businessman but you are not always going to succeed, but a good businessman won't quit just because he doesn't succeed. He will look for new avenues."*

### *Practice, Practice, Practice… Final Thoughts*

Even when we know intuitively that practicing will provide victories in our lives, we resist getting out on the field. Our reasons range from logical to highly emotional. We hug our excuses. Why? When I lived in New York, I developed the *Coney Island Theory of Life*, which states, " People would rather stay with what they know, even when it sucks, then make a change." Over time, I amended this theory to allow for wanting to change was one thing, changing was another and being able to change was a whole other thing again. By the time many of us step into reinvention of our lives, our past is so deeply imbedded in our beliefs, actions and results, that we have great difficulty making change. The condition we find ourselves is neither good nor bad; however, the longer we resist doing that which will ease our pain, the longer we suffer.

Distractions from pain make life more tolerable, but then we are constantly seeking a bigger better distraction to ease the discomfort. It's up to us to choose the kind of life and the kind of person we wish to be. I encourage people who engage in reinvention to begin dialoguing around the three elements discussed in this book. By the time we are reach adulthood, we are fairly entrenched in our personalities. A fall from grace is often a great time to review our lives. The window of opportunity sometimes stays open for a few days, or a few weeks, sometimes not. Falling or losing our footing in life will often result in our holding on more tightly to that which we know. Whether it's our logical minds justifying or rationalizing why life is the way it is, or our emotions barricading us or even our bodies burrowing into the earth for safety- letting go to free fall requires all the trust and courage we have.

I just hung up the phone with my friend Rick who has made great strides in changing his body, conditioning his physique. We share a common bond when it comes to weight loss and weight gain, falling off the wagon and getting back on again. At times, we have little faith that we will reach our goal. We practice kindness with each other because beating each other up would not yield any better results than the ones we currently experience. And we would feel worse about ourselves. The purpose in these conversations is to honestly acknowledge where we are with our program, provide feedback to each other, listen, listen, and listen.

Through the openings created with compassionate listening, we often find the next steps we need to take.

What link the three sides of the reinvention triangle together are love, patience and acceptance. Over time, Rick has learned to view himself with kindness, even when he does not score the big weight loss number he has set for himself. He just keeps getting back into the gym, reduces his intake of carbohydrates and tries again.

You can create an opportunity for Aha moments by having people participate in extraordinary transformational programs, but insight without action will not produce results. What enables us to move from awareness to action is practice. We don't like how vulnerable we feel when we deviate from a well- walked path. We don't know what is on the other side of how we have lived. We're afraid. Reinvention of the self is a continuous conversation. I've learned to respect and care for myself. The challenge is can we stay the path even when we don't see results? Reviewing my own frailties, my humanness, my propensity to hold onto my beliefs, has me walk a bit more softly around myself, a bit more softly around others. We are human beings after all. For every two steps forward, we take one step back. And that's okay!

## Gordon Graham- Soccer Hall of Fame 1997

*"Sports or business-- they are both competitive. If you want to go from here to there, you can get there if you are willing to learn, to listen, if you're willing to try. If there are twenty-four hours in a day, or however much time you are willing to give, you make the choice about how much energy you are willing to give".*

## *Practices Require Patience*

I grew up watching my grandmother darn socks. Using a small wooden block she would knit the sides of a hole together, deftly weaving wool until the hole completed disappeared. Although I didn't enjoy the time it took to darn socks, especially darning my father's size fourteen socks, I did enjoy watching the wooden block disappear as the wool formed a graft closing the open hole. Many years later, when I lived in Greece, I again had the opportunity to darn socks. This time around I used a potato as my backboard. I was not being coerced to darn. I actually enjoyed weaving the wool to graft the hole. I was not alone darning socks. I noticed how fishermen darned the sails of their boats as well as knitted their nets. They would sit for hours mending. Sometimes, they would sit close enough to one another on the docks so that they could spin yarns of the sea, their navy caps pushed high on their foreheads or low on their brows. Their hands moved quickly as their long needles glided in and out, in and out.

What was common among us was we had little funds to replace that which we owned. We made do with what we had, but we learned to how to keep improving or mending our tools so that we could continue to do our work.

We are no longer a darning society. We throw away that which has holes to start again. It's cheaper in the long run, we tell ourselves, to simply start over than it is to spend the time darning holes. We tell ourselves this about employees, relationships, even darning open holes in our lives. Although time consuming, darning left me with socks that lasted a lot longer than I anticipated. I am not suggesting that you all begin darning old socks. But I'm inviting you to look at practices that mend holes in yourself as worthwhile endeavors. How I approached darning changed as my attitude about the activity changed. I no longer saw darning as something obligatory. I made a choice that focused on the benefits of darning, not the task of darning. The practice calmed my nerves. My story sounds simple but oftentimes when we approach our practices as a way to calm our nerves, using the activity to address a problem, we will end up celebrating our results.

## Maureen Bunyan—News Anchor, Washington, DC

*"Sometimes you have to take the underlying themes that brought you success in a relationship or activity and apply them so you can blossom again. One of the themes of my life has been courage. I am not talking about the ability to do something; rather I am talking about a characteristic of my personality that allowed me to deal with a sick mother, and losing my mother as a child, going into a career in which women and minorities were not wanted. I know I am a courageous person. I can face fear because courage is the ability to face fear. I have the resources within myself. Other people have their themes that they can rely on and use to their utmost.*

*Maybe if we can accept the pain and the suffering in whatever form it comes, then we can be more fully human and maybe have a life more complete and more full. I think you have to be true yourself, whatever self you find. It's not just being responsible. It's learning about yourself and how to do that. You can do it introspectively; you can do it by learning from others. You can do it by having experiences. Through relationships, achievements and suffering. I want to be a whole person. I am searching to be authentic. I think it all gets back to how do you feel about yourself and how can you learn about yourself, wherever you find yourself."*

On Being Who I Am

*There is no greater moment*
*from which a man can rise*
*then the moment of inner peace*
*when the storm has lost its eye.*
*There is no greater safety*
*than a person straight and tall*
*who sees no need to guard his feed*
*because he has it all*
*he has it all within him*
*no more beggar nor knave to lie*
*and all his parts they fit him*
*no more need to question, "Why?"*

*Rhona Post 10/87*

# APPENDIX

# **COACHING EXERCISES**

**1.** What do I want my life to include?
_____
_____
_____
_____

**2.** What are the kinds of projects I would like to be doing?
_____
_____
_____
_____

**3.** What do I want my life to look like, to feel like?
_____
_____
_____
_____

**4.** What are the kinds of people or projects that zap my energy?
_____
_____
_____
_____

**5.** What have I done in the past that has made me happy?
_____
_____
_____
_____

**6.** If I had one year left to live, what would I do?
_____
_____
_____

**Ask Yourself:**

**1.** If you could paint your life, what elements would you include on the canvas?

_____
_____
_____
_____
_____

**2.** What images would the canvas hold?

_____
_____
_____
_____
_____

**3.** What mood(s) do you wish to portray on the canvas?

_____
_____
_____
_____
_____

**4.** Paint your life –whatever you paint is fine. Have fun.

**Ask Yourself:**
Journal This Question Daily. How will you know when you're doing the right thing or doing things right?

After four weeks of writing, ask yourself these five questions:

1. What have you learned about yourself in this process?

2. What actions, if any, can you begin taking that will help you close the gap between your ideal picture and your current reality?

3. What could get in the way?

4. What specific requests for help (and from whom) can you make now to close the gaps between where you are currently and where you wish to be?

**5.** Of the specific requests you outlined in Question #4, establish a timeline by when you will make your request..

**Instructions**: The key to this exercise is to see yourself at the end of your life, having accomplished your lifelong goals. From this resultant vantage point, answer the following questions:

**1.** What was worth accomplishing in your life?
_____
_____
_____
_____
_____

**2.** What were the specific qualities/traits required to achieve what you said was worth accomplishing?
_____
_____
_____
_____
_____

**3.** What were the specific projects you did to accomplish what you said was worth doing? (relates to question #1).
_____
_____
_____
_____
_____

**4.** What were the specific practices you did to develop/strengthen the qualities you identified in question #2?
_____
_____
_____
_____
_____

**Instructions:** Ask yourself the following questions in relationship to reinventing a particular system or structure. Customize as appropriate.

**1.** What do I/we need to do and for whom do we do it?

**2.** How well do we currently do what we do?

**3.** What do we need to improve, alter or change?

**4.** What are the outcomes of these changes? How will these changes affect us?

**5.** What's the impact of these changes on our relationships?

**6.** How can we best structure these changes so that they are made with the least amount of down time and instability?

_____
_____
_____
_____
_____

**7.** How will we know when the changes we have made meet our needs and our goals?

_____
_____
_____
_____
_____

**Instructions:** You have the vision of what is worth doing. You have outlined systems or structures that will support you to bring your vision to life. Now identify the skills you will need to tie the package together.

1. Identify one area of your life that you believe is worth improving or enhancing as it relates to your overall dream of how you want your life to look.

   _____
   _____
   _____
   _____
   _____

2. What it's going to take in terms of time, money and resources to accomplish your goal?

   _____
   _____
   _____
   _____
   _____

3. What specific skills will you need to succeed?

   _____
   _____
   _____
   _____
   _____

4. What do you already know (knowledge) that you can apply?

   _____
   _____
   _____
   _____
   _____

5. What's missing in your knowledge base that if you had the information would move you forward to achieve?

   _____
   _____

_____
_____
_____

**6.** Who or what sources are available from whom you can learn or apprentice?
_____
_____
_____
_____
_____

**7.** What outcomes are you seeking from spending time or money to learn what you need?
_____
_____
_____
_____
_____

## *ACKNOWLEDGMENTS:*

I'd like to acknowledge the lessons my mother taught us, including the phrase: *"There is no such word as can't."*

I also want to thank the following people for freely and lovingly giving their time, and support to this project:

**Victoria Heland**- the Best writer's midwife on the East Coast. She skillfully helped me give birth to this book.

**Walter Gavin**- my muse. From the beginning, he told me I could write a book. Walt provided great catchy chapter titles.

**Lou Briganti**- Big Train Marketing. "Just Do It!" he said.

**James Flaherty-** CEO of New Ventures West who introduced me to coaching and to this three -step tool. I found my calling.

Thank you to the many people who gave their time to be interviewed as I researched the three-step reinvention tool. You generously shared your stories, feelings and spirit. During each interview, I'd feel a surge of energy when we connected to what mattered to you; your quotes are sprinkled liberally throughout this workbook. I especially want to acknowledge my friend, **Probyn Thomps**on and his family for meeting with me the day after they buried his wife.

## *Acknowledgments To Book Contributors*

I interviewed a wide range of people because I knew that I was not alone in my feelings about loss and change. Each time I tackled a new section of the book, I would meet men and women whose life and work experiences strengthened my commitment to writing. To all those people whose lives touched mine and whose support enabled me to either access some of the interviewees, or whose guidance led me to re-think how I wanted to present my ideas, I want to thank you, again.

*Navigating Tomorrow* is a book that belongs to all of us.

**Probyn Thompson, Sr.**
**Lt. Col. Probyn Thompson, III.**
**Mary Thompson**
**Meg Reggie**, Atlanta Magazine
**Vincent Coppla**, Atlanta
**Maureen Bunyan**, Washington DC. Television Anchorperson
**James Flaherty**, CEO and Founder of New Ventures West
**Rickie Calvin Harris**, NFL retired
**Fran O'Brien**, NFL retired/deceased
**Alvin E. Hall, Sr.**, EG&G
**Melissa McNair Bennett**, Integrative Life Practices, Inc.
**Frank Hall**, networked me to **Barbara Roberts**, **Mike Dukakis** and **Gordon Graham**
**Gordon Bradley**, Soccer Hall of Fame
**Archie Manning**, NFL retired
**Leonard J. Elmore**, NBA retired
**Woody Fitzhugh** Senior PGA Professional
**Dr. Frank Jenkins**, networked me to **Huey Richardson**.
**Huey Richardson**, NFL
**Reid Falwell**, Daring mountain climber
**Moody R. Tidwell**, Judge, Retired, US Federal Claims Court
**William Dennis Turner**, Golden Gloves, ex-convict, now free
**Nina Totenberg**, Legal Affairs Correspondent, National Public Radio
**Vicki Heeland**, Heland & Heland Communication.
**Walter Harris Gavin**, muse, editor and cheerleader.
**Richard Barnett**, PhD, NBA retired

**Manny Lopes**, who introduced me to **Dr. Richard Barnett**.
**Betty Porter,** Assistant Director Committee on Equal Employment: Kennedy Administration, White House Speechwriter for Kennedy
**Richard Stratton**, Publisher of Prison Life Magazine
**Gary Green**, Youngest NHL Coach, Sports Commentator
**Donna Lopiano**, Women's Sports Foundation
**Barbara Roberts**, Governor of Oregon
**Mike Dukakis**, Governor of Massachusetts
**Carole Crumbley**, Reverend, National Washington Cathedral, DC, Shambala Institute
**Ben Nighthorse Campbell**, Senator: Colorado
**Bruce Lehman**, Commissioner US Patent and Trademark Office, Clinton Administration
**Lou Briganti**, Big Train Marketing
**Kathy Wilson**, Australian Pro Basketball, College Womens' Basketball Coach
**Mitchell Johnson**, NFL retired
**Richard Goodstein**, Advanced Certified Rolfer

## ABOUT THE AUTHOR

### Rhona Post, The Healer Coach
www.thehealercoach.com

Rhona Post, author, radio personality, an International Coach Federation (ICF) master certified coach since 1999, has traversed the landscape of professional coaching, with certifications and continued study in ontological and somatic coaching and most recently, Core Individuation, the use of energetic healing to guide clients to wholeness: mind, body, spirit and emotions.

More than 30 years ago, Ms. Post began studying personal/leadership development with such luminaries as Werner Erhard, John Hanley, James Flaherty and Julio Ollaha. She advanced her national practice by working with diverse groups of leaders, managers and employees, both in the private and public sectors. Most recently, Ms. Post established a Management coaching program at NASA's Goddard Space Flight Center. She helped managers and employees better understand how their body language impacted communication. As a result, coaching clients learned to lead with their head and heart resulting in improved customer relations, and workplace morale.

In 2009, Ms. Post changed her company name to The Healer Coach LLC representing the intersection of her mindfulness practice, energy work and somatic coaching. She teaches other coaches how to incorporate the healing arts in their coaching practice. She also maintains an international healer coaching practice working with individuals and groups who want to experience inner peace and more joy. As part of her commitment to empowering others to lead the life they dream, she has started a Straight Talk network of coaching programs dealing with aging, sex and dating, for women and the men who love them.

www.ingramcontent.com/pod-product-compliance
Lightning Source LLC
Chambersburg PA
CBHW041616220426
43671CB00001B/5